Approaching Integral Mission

Approaching Integral Mission

John Wibberley

E. John Wibberley

AFRICA CHRISTIAN TEXTBOOKS

2021

Approaching Integral Mission
© 2021 ACTS and NACREN

Africa Christian Textbooks (ACTS)

ACTS Bookshop, International HQ, TCNN,
PMB 2020, Bukuru, Plateau State, 930008, Nigeria
GSM: +234 (0) 803-589-5328; E-mail: pa@actsnigeria.org
Website: http://actsnigeria.org

ISBN: 978-978-905-500-5 Print

Cover Design: Billy Abwa
Illustrations: Michael Huggins
Book Design: Gustavo Mena

Contents

FOREWORD

I am really excited about the impact of this book *Approaching Integral Mission*. When the church is committed to *Integral Mission*, it will incarnate the values of the Kingdom of God and witness to God's love and the justice revealed through Jesus Christ.

Peter Batchelor (1926-2016) took his Christian faith seriously to be applied in practice to every aspect of life, and believed this should be shared accordingly. Thus he was led to spend his life engaged in integral mission, founding *Faith & Farm* in Nigeria in 1958, becoming an early trustee of *Tearfund* UK from 1968, and co-founding *RURCON Africa* in 1971. The late Bishop Simon Barrington Ward KCMG speaking in 2008 to RURCON Communications Unit UK Trustees & Advisory Council of which he was Chairman for 30 years from 1980-2010, said:

> Integral mission is to help people to make their corporate dwelling with Christ for fullness of life now, so that all of it is transformed (farming and so on), so that Jesus Christ will be found and find them again and again.

Integral Mission enables the church to bring a prophetic word, addressing the whole person, including their physical, social and spiritual needs. By the power of the Holy Spirit, this leads to transformation at all levels - individual, family and community. The task of the local church is to *equip and mobilise men and women for God's mission - integral mission*, not exclusively in the church building, but in ways that will honour the Lordship of Jesus Christ throughout all the diverse fields of human endeavour.

Andrew Gwaivangmin,
Executive Secretary of Nigeria Evangelical Missions Association (NEMA) & former Team Leader/CEO of RURCON Africa.

ACKNOWLEDGMENTS

Countless people have enabled the compilation of this short handbook – many of them unwittingly by their practical home, church and farmstead demonstrations, by their words and writings, from home and early life onwards. Some references and further readings are listed at the end but this is by no means exhaustive, nor is this book an academic treatise. It is intended to suggest Biblically-grounded guidelines for Integral Mission planning, discussion and implementation in practice. In particular, I owe to the late Peter Batchelor (1926-2016) the specific articulation and outworking of Integral Mission Principles via Faith & Farm and RURCON Africa (began 1971) – and inspiration from colleagues: the late Barnaba Dusu, Sulaiman Jakonda, Bishop Simon Barrington-Ward, Karimu Damap, Danladi Musa, Mike Oye, Eunice Pwol in Nigeria; continued encouragement to compile this book by Andrew Gwaivangmin, and support of Sam Ishaya, John Horton, John Fowler, David & Betty Payne, Stephen Stordy, Obed Dashan; Thanks also to:- Tom Ahima, Florence Yeboah of Ghana; Gladys Mwiti of Kenya; Siaka Charles of Sierra Leone; the late Godwin Chetti of Tanzania; Grace Kyeyune, the late Frank Rwakabwohe, the late Elijah Kyamuwendo, Richard Tumushabe of Uganda. I thank Jennie Evans, the late Ian Wallace, Simon Webley, formerly of Tearfund UK; Bishop Stephen & Rael Kewasis & team of Kenya; Von van der Linde & the late Gerald Dedekind of ACAT, RSA; Michael Cassidy, David Peters of African Enterprise RSA; Glenn & Verna Schwartz of USA; Elbert van Donkersgoed of Canada; Solomon & Ruth Nabie & Team of IcFEM, Kenya; Martin & Julia Etter, Malawi; Souleymane Anne, Gaston Slanwa in Niger; Lambert Kouboubé in Cameroon; Fikre Norcha in Ethiopia. Friends who have discussed matters of integral mission over many years and encouraged me in it include Alan Backhurst, Andrew Edmunds, Mike Graveney, Anthony Herbert, Michael & Pauline Huggins (Michael kindly provided use of his own drawings here), Christopher & Ita Jones, Peter Kent, David & Susie Ursell. My wife Jane is ever wholly supportive, as is our family. May the Lord use this offered distillation of integral mission experience, and may it be clear that its shortcomings are mine. Warm thanks are accorded to Sid Garland and the ACTS Team.

INTRODUCTION

This short book offers some pointers for discussion and application in the context of advice, training, education, advocacy and resource management through Churches, Christian and Community Organisations on practical issues related to Integral Mission for Wholistic Development. Wholistic Development means "God-defined progress of *whole* people - body, mind and spirit - in *whole* relationships - UP to God, OUT to other people and DOWN to the earth context in which our life is set." It stresses *enabling* through local self-reliance and practical resource management for sustainable lifestyles based on good christian stewardship or "Caring Management," focusing on the poor and needy but including others and enabling enterprise. It arose from practice, is not an academic treatise nor can it possibly acknowledge the many whose actions, words and wisdom have generously helped to formulate its proposed approach to integral mission. The author accepts all responsibility for any omissions and errors in its compilation.

A particular comment about integral mission that thrilled me was from an African farmer who said, with a radiant smile on her face, "Now we can use our own hands for our own development!"

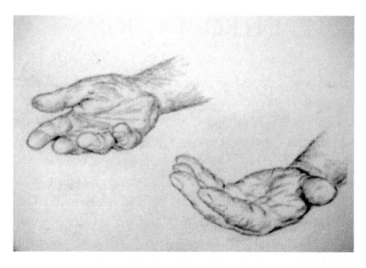

The "textbooks" for integral mission are the Bible – God's Word, and creation – spoken into being and sustained by God. It is argued that these "books" should be "read" *together* as we seek under God to serve the cause of integral mission for wholistic development.

This book draws on the author's experience and involvement in development practice in Africa, Asia, Europe, the Middle East, the Americas, and Oceania. However, much of the original inspiration and experience shared in this book was derived through working with RURCON (covering Rural and Urban Resources; Counselling, Outreach and Networking), a small Pan-African team of Christian leaders offering service for wholistic community development through Christian Churches in Africa. With the late Da Barnaba Dusu, RURCON's Founder Chairman, RURCON was started in 1971 by the late Peter Batchelor (1926-2016), a missionary serving in Nigeria with Sudan United Mission (now part of *Pioneer* UK). He had previously begun *Faith* and *Farm* in 1958, also in Nigeria, in response to the needs of agricultural development in the context of the whole gospel for the whole person and community. The present writer first met Peter when he addressed an Agricultural Christian Fellowship Group of students at the University of Reading in 1966. Among other things, he spoke about the basis of properly hygienic simple latrines by reference to Deut.23:12-13 and explained that the Bible is a very practical book that shows Jesus Christ's concern for the body, mind and soul working together now and towards eternity. The realities of African pre-Christian cultures are of religions fully-integrated with everyday life such that the ancestors operate as the *living dead* and are consulted in all matters pertaining to farming and other practical lifestyle and livelihood decisions. By contrast, the Christian gospel to be spread through Integral Mission is based on a risen Saviour, The Lord Jesus Christ, with an empty cross coupled with an empty tomb, and requires us to *put ourselves on the cross and die to self* as Paul told Galatians 2:20: *I am crucified with Christ, nevertheless I live, yet not I but Christ lives in me.* A chart used in many workshops is at Fig.1.

Figure 1. The Cross & Relationships

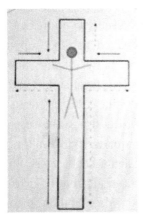

The cross and empty tomb are rather like the old Cyrillic symbol ҍ. The cross points upwards to God, outwards to neighbours and downwards to earth. It symbolises mutual relationships: from and to God (in blessings received and worship returned); to and from neighbours (in service/help given and received); to and from earth (in stewardship or caring management given, and produce for life and livelihoods received).

Figure 2. The Cross & Integral mision

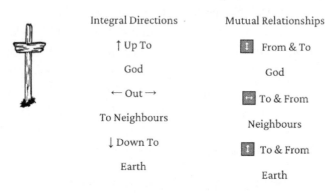

Integral Directions   Mutual Relationships

↑ Up To   From & To

God   God

← Out →   To & From

To Neighbours   Neighbours

↓ Down To   To & From

Earth   Earth

The gospel, as often presented, addresses personal salvation - a personal "ticket to heaven" or the "upward" dimension - but not enough towards the matter of the "horizontal" dimension of relationships with others (our neighbours), and very little towards the "downward" dimension of the earth, its creatures and its stewardship. *Faith and Farm* sought to address these issues - working directly with older farmers rather than relying on the hope of "trickle down" from agriculturally-educated school-leavers. Rural African cultures are gerontocracies – with power and control increasing with age, coupled with due respect for one's elders. In those circumstances, change tends to start with persuading older people first. *Faith and Farm* provided linkages between faith and everyday life (i.e. a Biblical gospel, which is wholistic was preached and practiced). RURCON began in 1971 in response to requests from churches, organisations and communities for help in replicating the sort of work done by *Faith and Farm* elsewhere in Africa, beginning with a request from Pastor David Telta in Chad.

RURCON operates Africa-wide and has worked in some 35 countries of sub-Saharan Africa. It is interdenominational in its membership and focus, and seeks to be both responsive to church requests for help and pro-active in furthering the cause through education and extension of appropriate ideas, values and practices. RURCON Headquarters is in Jos, Nigeria and has been led there by Peter Batchelor, the late Sulaiman Jakonda, the late Karimu Damap, Andrew Gwaivangmin and then Sam Ishaya (www.rurcon.net) with regional groups of countries - both Anglophone and Francophone - served in West, East, Southern and Central Africa. RURCON has sought to facilitate the formation of National Christian Development Associations (CDAs) - such as CDASL (in Sierra Leone) - to act as Communication Points for information, networking and concerted action in furtherance of the work of the Kingdom of God. RURCON believes God made us to be givers and receivers in *relationship* with Him, with each other and with our particular place and resources. RURCON focuses on *people and possessions engaged in prayerful progress* using appropriate ideas and technology - for water development, farming, health, shelter, transport and all the interlinked aspects of daily realities.

Success in RURCON's work of promoting christian stewardship can be assessed by several outcome criteria, including:

- greater trust in God the Father, Son and Holy Spirit as people of integrity (Psalm 86:11);
- greater fellowship together - stronger communities, with improved relationships between those of any faith and none (Mt.5:9);

- greater harnessing of resources for local benefit, for God's work locally and to give away.

Proverbs 29:18 warns *where there is no vision, the people perish;* the corollary is that where there is vision, the work of God can flourish. To have a project, programme or plan, however well prepared, is no guarantee of success in genuine development without humble dependence on the Spirit of God in its conception and execution, and without discernment to avoid false teachings and false goals – as Jesus Himself warned (Matthew 24:24-25).

Christian stewardship is central to the progress of the church since Christians are stewards of:

- the gospel (good news) of Jesus Christ and his cross
- ourselves - souls, minds and bodies with their unique time and talents
- others around us - their souls, minds and bodies
- whatever material resources and equipment God entrusts to us
- the environment - to ensure sustainable livelihoods in future for all, and those yet unborn – *occupying until the Lord returns* (Luke 19:13).

RURCON does **not** run projects – believing that local people need to take responsibility - but rather, advises and trains on christian stewardship for development to alleviate the vicious cycle of rural poverty (Fig.3).

Figure 3. The Vicious Cycle of Rural Poverty

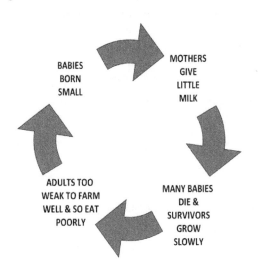

Isaiah 58:6-11 expresses God's aspirations for integral mission:

> *Is not this the fast that I have chosen? –to loose the bands of*
> *wickedness, to undo the heavy burdens, and to let the oppressed go*
> *free, and that you break every yoke? Is it not to deal your bread to the*
> *hungry, and that you bring the poor who are cast out to your house?*
> *– when you see the naked , that you cover him; and that you do not*
> *hide yourself from your own flesh? Then shall your light break forth*
> *as the morning and your health shall spring forth speedily…*

RURCON since 1971 seeks to help churches, organisations, individuals
and whole communities in Africa to be effective stewards of God's
earth through training and mobilisation. The aim is to *optimise*
resources for "enough" (Fig.4).

**Figure 4. "Enough" = Balanced Optima
rather than maximal or minimal.**

Maximise	Optimise	Minimise
Transnational	Local integrated	Isolationist
Limitless	Boundaries	Blinkered
Exhaustion	Sustainability	Stagnation
Greed & debt	Needs met	Shortages
Obesity	Sufficiency	Malnourishment
Exploitation	Integral	Neglect

Chapter 1

The Content of Integral Mission

The Vocation Of Integral Mission

Integral Mission is a vocation – a calling to serve God in line with Biblical principles. It is not a technique of mission strategy but a calling. Christians are called by God as he softens our hearts and challenges our minds and spirits to move from darkness into his marvellous light, and to team with others who aspire to become his disciples by grace. Biblical discipleship involves seeking to understand God's Word by the inspiration and interpretation of his Holy Spirit and then *apply* it to all aspects of personal, family, community, national and international living. First, then, in order to engage in integral mission we must die to self. Paul said (Gal.2:20) *I am crucified with Christ nevertheless I live, yet not I but Christ lives in me.* From that position, one's spirit is made alive to worship and bring pleasure to God as well as to receive from him his blessings in a personal, dynamic way. One's spirit is enlivened towards one's neighbour in practical loving interaction, both giving and receiving help in that way through interdependence. Furthermore, an often neglected aspect of integral mission by some otherwise keen Bible-esteeming churches is towards the earth and all its creatures from which we derive livelihoods and sustenance for life on earth and towards which we are called to exercise responsible Christian stewardship (caring management). Fig.1 above seeks to encapsulate the above definitions. To be equipped for integral mission, we need to be re-shaped by our loving creator God like clay in the hands of the potter (Jer.18:4-6). Integral Mission may lead us to dangerous places as per the postcard found among my late grandfather's possessions from World War 1 in Passchendaele (Fig.5).

Figure 5. Shaped and Prepared for Integral Mission service

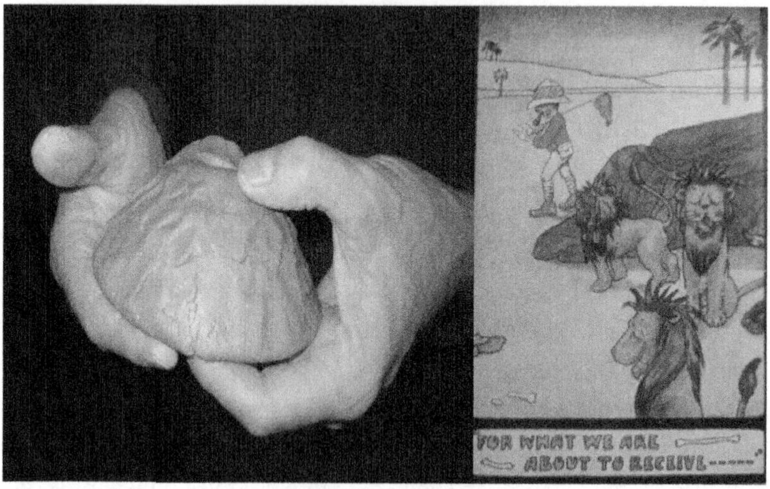

FOR WHAT WE ARE
ABOUT TO RECEIVE

Customs, Culture & Christianity

It is essential that we take time to seek understanding of any culture in which we are engaged in integral mission. This is required for three reasons:

a.   To understand how the people think, feel and understand the world around them
b.   To express the changeless gospel of Christ in terms that translate culturally. There is a redemptive analogy that fits every culture. Jesus Himself used this via parables.

c.   To avoid unnecessarily offending cultural norms as Paul advised, *If possible live at peace with everyone* (Rom.12:18). Therefore, "behave properly"!

Figure 6. All cultures operate at four levels

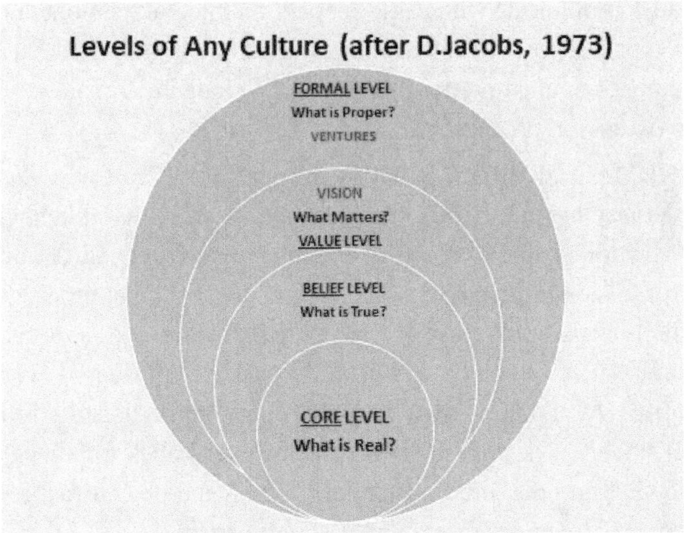

Levels of Any Culture (after D.Jacobs, 1973)

FORMAL LEVEL
What is Proper?
VENTURES

VISION
What Matters?
VALUE LEVEL

BELIEF LEVEL
What is True?

CORE LEVEL
What is Real?

- **CORE LEVEL** = the very heart of a person's reality. We need to ask, "What is real?" As a child, I recall being convinced there was a thief under my bed one night; instead of just laughing at me, my father shone a torch to show me this was untrue! A disciple is someone who has been changed "to the core." If Christ is to occupy the throne of a person's life, then what is there already has to be brought to light and ultimately dethroned.
- **BELIEF LEVEL** = What is true for a person? What do they believe is true now? For instance, I met someone deep in the bush who was convinced that the world is flat and found my spherical globe meaningless at first. Truth is crucial – which is why Jesus claimed

He embodies not only the way, but also the truth, and the life (John 14:6).

- **VALUE LEVEL** = What matters to a person? What do they deeply value? For the Maasai in East Africa, cattle are highly prized - as they are among all pastoralist communities worldwide. To work and communicate with cattle keepers, an integral missioner needs to appreciate cows! Many cultures value freedom so highly that they ignore communal needs at the expense of individual claimed rights to do as one pleases.

- **FORMAL LEVEL** = What is proper? Some cultures elevate tolerance to such a level that false and even immoral behaviour is condoned in the name of tolerance. However, all ethnically proscribed cultures have their own norms for greeting. Eskimos (Inuit people) rub noses on meeting. Each culture uses a distinctive combination of words and gestures that are considered "correct form." An integral missioner needs to learn these early and sensitively. The formal level also includes codes for dress and clothing, and the sort of vision for business and other activities that are considered desirable or at least permissible.

The late Donald Jacobs imparted to me this categorisation of culture levels almost five decades ago and I have found it very useful in helping others to describe key features of their own cultures as a prelude to discussing both extension approaches and helpful preaching content. There are those who dangerously start their teaching and preaching by seeking to 'chime with the culture' to adapt to the culture in ways that dilute the truth of the Bible. The desire to 'attract' people into churches and Christian gatherings persuades some to use methods that mimic the world of fantasy and popular culture. The genuine integral missioner will start with the Bible and seek to impart its truth in full as God's Word but expressing it in terms that are comprehensible to those hearing it.

The coming of Jesus Christ into someone's life transforms it. This was evident when early missionaries arrived among tribes whose practices included such things as body-piercing, and tattoos. It is a mark of the fashions of much modern behaviour as seen worldwide in the media that many have reverted to these same practices often with ugly results which are contrary to the Bible (Lev.19:28). Some of those who turn to Christ go to further expense to have removed unsuitable tattoos which they now regret. These matters need discussing sensitively but openly with youth groups in particular.

God's Discipleship Development Goals

On a hilltop in Devon, UK is a huge broken rock on which are engraved the words of the ten commandments – as found in Exodus 20:1-17. These are found written on the walls in many churches where young and old alike can read, learn and inwardly digest them. They supply all humans with "The Maker's Instructions" for a blessed and fruitful life and harmonious society (*I am the LORD your God* says Ex.20:1-2). Just as the manufacturer of a vehicle specifies how it should be run and serviced, so God has done for our benefit - as our maker who intends our total well-being (Psa.119:1-16). We defy them at our peril and loss. We are to promote them within integral mission. The ten commandments (orders for life) are as follows:

1. *No other gods: You shall have no other gods before me* (Ex.20:3)
2. *No idols: You shall not make for yourself an image in the form of anything* ..(Ex.20:4-6)
3. *No swearing: You shall not misuse the name of the LORD your God* (Ex.20:7)

4. *Keep Sabbath: Remember the Sabbath day by keeping it holy....* (Ex.20:8-11)
5. *Honour parents: Honour your father and your mother* (Ex.20:12)
6. *No killing: You shall not murder* (Ex.20:13)
7. *No adultery: You shall not commit adultery* (Ex.20:14)
8. *No theft: You shall not steal* (Ex.20:15)
9. *No false witness: You shall not give false testimony against your neighbour* (Ex.20:16)
10. *No covetousness: You shall not covert your neighbour's house* (Ex.20:17).

If we kept to these straightforward instructions from God, our news bulletins would be vastly different, and our lives so much less confused, and so much more contented and peaceful. May the Lord help us to so live to his glory, and to so advocate through integral mission.

Then we are to train up others for the task. Paul's instructions to Timothy are very pertinent here regarding passing on truth. In this way a sort of relay race of disciples is set up inter-generationally. *..entrust to reliable people who will also be qualified to teach others.* Paul goes on to say,

> *Do your best to present yourself to God as one approved, a workman who does not need to be ashamed and who correctly handles the word of truth*
>
> $-$2 Tim.2:2,15

Sustainable Development Goals: A ChristianResponse

The SDGs (Sustainable Development Goals) of 2015 build on those established at the Millennium (MDGs) and address global challenges, including those related to poverty, inequality, climate, environmental degradation, prosperity, peace and justice. The 17 Sustainable Development Goals of 2015 interconnect and their attainment is aspired by 2030. The Sustainable Development Goals (SDGs) are:

1. End poverty in all its forms everywhere.
2. End hunger, achieve food security & improved nutrition & promote sustainable agriculture.
3. Ensure healthy lives and promote well-being for all at all ages.
4. Ensure inclusive, equitable, quality education & promote lifelong learning opportunities for all.
5. Achieve gender equality and empower all women and girls.
6. Ensure availability and sustainable management of water and sanitation for all.
7. Ensure access to affordable, reliable, sustainable and modern energy for all.
8. Promote sustained, inclusive and sustainable economic growth, full and productive employment and decent work for all.
9. Build resilient infrastructure, promote inclusive & sustainable industrialisation & foster innovation.
10. Reduce inequality within and among countries.
11. Make cities and human settlements inclusive, safe, resilient and sustainable.
12. Ensure sustainable consumption and production patterns.
13. Take urgent action to combat climate change and its impacts.
14. Conserve & sustainably use oceans, seas & marine resources for sustainable development.
15. Protect, restore & promote sustainable use of terrestrial ecosystems, sustainably manage forests, combat desertification, and halt & reverse land degradation and halt biodiversity loss.

16. Promote peaceful and inclusive societies for sustainable development, provide access to justice for all and build effective, accountable and inclusive institutions at all levels.
17. Strengthen the means of implementation & revitalise global partnership for sustainable development.

The Millennium Development Goals (MDGs) covered eight aspects more concisely:

1. **Eradicate Extreme Poverty And Hunger**
   - Isa. 58 – especially vv.6-14
   - *You give them something to eat* said Jesus (Mark 6:37)
   - Still almost 1 billion of earth's 8 billion were hungry in 2020
2. **Achieve Universal Primary Education (Upe)**
   - *Remember your Creator in the days of your youth* (Ecclesiastes 12:1)
   - *Start children off on the way they should go* (Proverbs 22:6)
3. **Promote Gender Equality And Empower Women**
   - *God does not show favouritism* (Acts 10:34)
   - *for you are all one in Christ Jesus* (Galatians 3:28)
4. **Reduce Child Mortality**
   - *Let the little children come to me....* (Matt. 19:14a)
   - Luke 1:59 – 8th day circumcision, date by which blood can clot with K+
5. **Improve Maternal Health**
   - Isa.49:15 *Can a mother forget the baby at her breast?*
   - Isa.54:5 – *For your Maker is your husband...*
6. **Combat HIV/Aids, Malaria And Other Diseases**
   - Marriage – instituted, honoured and defended
   - *I will not bring on you any of the diseases ...* (conditional – Exodus 15:26; Deut.7:15)

7. **Ensure Environmental Sustainability**
    - *...in the Garden of Eden to work it and take care of it.* (Gen.1;26-28; 2:15)
    - dominion = authority to rule according to God's wishes (Psalm 150:6)

8. **Develop Global Partnership For Development**
    - *For we are fellow workers in God's service...* (1 Cor.3:9)
    - *God sets the lonely in families* (Psa.68:6)

Chapter 2

The Centrality of Christ

Who Did Jesus Christ Say/Explain He Is?

Very truly I tell you John 3:3,11	I have power to die and rise again Jn.10:18
I am He (Messiah) John 4:25,26	I am the Son of God John 10:24,25
Very truly I tell you John 5:19,24,25	*I and the Father are one* John 10:30,36-38
Very truly I tell you John 6:26	**I am the resurrection & the life** John 11:25
I am "God-sent" from heaven John 6:29,33	*Very truly I tell you* John 12:24-26
I am the bread of life John 6:35, 48, 51	*You [rightly] call me "Teacher" and "Lord"* John 13:13
Very truly I tell you John 6:47,53	*Very truly I tell you* Jn. 13:16,20,21,38
I will raise them up John 6:40,44,54	**I am the way and the truth and the life.** John 14:6

...you are the Holy One of God. Jn 6:69	*I am in the Father/the Father in Me* Jn.14:10
...he who sent me is true. John 7:28,29	*I am in my Father/you in me/I in you* Jn.14:20
Let anyone who is thirsty come to me and drink Jn.7:37,38	**I am the true vine** John 15:1
I am the light of the world John 8:12	*I am the vine, you are the branches* John 15:5
I am not alone. I stand with the Father, who sent me. John 8:16	*When the Advocate comes....* John 15:26
I am from above ... not of this world Jn.8:23	*Very truly I tell you* John 16:7, 20
before Abraham was born, I am. John 8:58	*I will send him [Holy Spirit or Advocate] to you* John 16:7
'f you hold to my teaching.... you will know the truth, and the truth will set you free. John 8:31 - 32,36	*But when ... the Spirit of truth, comes, ... he will glorify me ...* John 16:13,14
Very truly I tell you John 8:34	*Very truly I tell you* John 21:18
I have come here from God John 8:42	*I am Jesus, whom you are persecuting* Acts 9:5
Very truly I tell you Jn.8:45,46,51, 58	*I am Jesus of Nazareth, whom you are persecuting* Acts 22:8
*Before Abraham was, **I am*** John 8:58	*I am Jesus, whom you are persecuting* Acts 26:15
I am the light of the world John 9:5	*I am the Alpha and the Omega, the First and the Last.....* Rev.1:8;22:13

For judgment I have come into this world John 9:39	I am alive for ever and ever Rev.1:18
Very truly I tell you John 10:1	I am coming soon! Rev.22:7,12
I am the gate Jn.10:7,9	I am the Root & the Offspring of David Rev.22:16
I am the good shepherd John 10:11,14	I am coming soon! Rev.22:20

An old hymn by *George Washington Doane* (1799-1859) puts it all well:

Thou art the Way: to Thee alone from sin and death we flee:
And he who would the Father seek, must seek Him Lord by Thee.

Thou art the Truth: Thy Word alone true wisdom can impart;
Thou only canst inform the mind and purify the heart.

Thou art the Life: the rending tomb proclaims Thy conquering arm;
And those who put their trust in Thee nor death nor hell shall harm.

Thou art the Way, the Truth, the Life; grant us that Way to know,
That Truth to keep, that Life to win, whose joys eternal flow.

Why & How Jesus Alone is Supreme

1. Co-Creator with God the Father & the Holy Spirit who love all they made (Gen.1:26,27; Jn.1:1-4).
2. Eternal pre-existent One who was and is and is to come, in charge of all things (Heb.1:1-3; 13:8).

3.   Truly God and truly man by Virgin Birth (Isa.7:14; Matt.1:18-23).

4.   Sole route between earth and heaven (John 14:6; Rev.22:13-21).

5.   Saviour by his blood shed once and for all (Jn.3:16,17; Acts 20:28; Eph.2:13; 1 Peter 1:18,19).

6.   Propitiation for our sin = cleansing & atonement reconciling us to God by faith (Rom.3:25; 1 Jn.2:2).

7.   Sustainer by his risen life (Gal.2:20,21; Col.1:15-19).

8.   Victor over death through his resurrection (1 Cor.15:54-58; 1 Jn.5:4-12).

9.   Conqueror of Satan (Rev.12:9-12; 15:2; 20:10).

10. Hope of the world through his return (Acts 1:11; Acts 17:23-31; Rev.19:11-16).

11. Great Shepherd of his sheep (Psa.23; Jn.10:11,14; Heb.13:20,21).

12. Nearest kinsman & supreme valuer of souls (Mk.8:35-38; 1 Peter 4:19).

Discipleship: Growing in Christ to Maturity

For believers, discipleship – growing in Christ to maturity – is a lifelong journey (pilgrimage). It is enabled by the combination of Word (Bible & Christ the Living Word) with Spirit (Holy Spirit guidance – John 16:13-15) and the vital discernment (which is a gift of that self-same Spirit to warn us of falsehood. Discipleship is God's agenda for all believers. It is the purpose of the Great Commission spoken by Jesus to his disciples in Matthew 28:18-20:

> *All authority in heaven and on earth has been given to me. Therefore go and make disciples of all nations, baptising them in the name of the Father and of the Son and of the Holy Spirit, and teaching them to obey everything I have commanded you. And surely I am with you always, to the very end of the age.*

The task is not simply to make converts but disciples – those who apply their faith in Christ practically to all aspects of their lives; that is to say who operate as integral missioners both at home and away!

Integrity: Meditation & Behaviour for Believer & Church

Becoming a true believer means substituting complete reliance on Christ where self-reliance once ruled (Acts 16:31). The transaction involves what Paul expresses in Gal. 2:20: *I have been crucified with Christ, and I no longer live, but Christ lives in me.* Discipleship involves surrendering oneself as an integral whole being – body, mind and spirit – to Christ so that one's heart is the wellspring of love towards God (Prov.4:23) and one's will seeks to be obedient to him (Phil.2:1-11). God intends by design a state of integrity within one's being, and of relationship to God, to neighbours, and to our earth context. Satan's agenda is to disintegrate the believer's being and that of the church – *the thief comes only to steal and kill and destroy* whereas Jesus came *that [we] may have life, and have it to the full.* (John 10:9,10).

How does Satan pursue his agenda of disintegration?

a.   Satan peddles the lie that one can separate the body from the mind and from the spirit.

b.   With this, he peddles Gnosticism (secret knowledge) and multiple "New Age" ideas and practices.

c.   Satan peddles a variety of "techniques" for manipulating the body, the mind or the spirit in isolation.

d.   For the body, this leads to exploitation/obsessive concern about looks, muscle-tone.

e.   For the mind, the "mindfulness" movement is fashionable (it depends on whether what is in the mind derives from God and the Bible or not); mental health dysfunctions – and all that will promote them; Transcendental Meditation (TM) is an old and dangerous fallacy whereby the subject is invited to empty one's mind and see what pops back in guided by a veiled form of Hindu Yoga, popularised by Maharishi Mahesh Yogi and Ayurveda products, now peddled as "stress therapy." Jesus warned about this sort of occurrence and its results in Luke 11:24-26.

f.   For the spirit, the concept of spirituality as a commodity, worship as musical mantras. Beware these teachings and the "pedigree" of the "stables" from which they originate.

g.   Combined substitutes for normal godliness include practices such as yoga, Pilates, nature worship... Pilates is a form of exercise developed by Joseph Pilates in the early 1900s. Weak when a child, he studied body-building, yoga, qigong, and gymnastics, combining the different practices into one "contrology" system based on breathing in relation to physical exertion. Ignorant of its origins, many Christians appear to have adopted the fad – which is described as "non-religious" (by contrast with yoga) but given its sometimes negative physiological effects, why not use straightforward exercise instead – walking, swimming, simple physical exercises and contemplating the wonders of God's creation?

h.   Satan plays with human laziness, as per "The Devil finds work for idle hands to do..."

Much money is made by various false prophets (1 John 4:1-3) peddling a cocktail of these therapies, including repetitive *sozo* "counselling" and classes on the above. Not all labelled "alternative therapies" are to be shunned or avoided as potentially harmful – or at best a waste of money. To do so would miss good natural remedies based on plant sources, cod liver oil etc (many are good, though some of these may be administered by "quack" doctors or with exorbitant claims as to their efficacy; some may be given along with "spiritist" overtones by witchdoctors). Wholesome use of God's natural remedies such as dock leaves for nettle stings during the normal exercise of walking around fields is to be encouraged (see for instance www.anamed.org).

How may the Christian pursue an agenda ofintegrity?

a. Meditate on (ruminate, chew over) God's **Word** – comparing scripture with scripture.

b. Cultivate your loving **relationship** with God: we only love because he first loved us (1 Jn.4:7-21). Love from God is *agape* – a quality and depth of love we can only show by his gift of the Holy Spirit living/behaving within us.

c. Pray in the **Spirit** day-by-day: see God more clearly, love him more dearly, follow him more nearly (the Prayer of St Richard of Chichester).

d. Take time to enjoy and receive the **blessing** of God's **creation** along with him.

e. Periodically review & pursue **balance** (or otherwise) of your diet, diary, media exposure, priorities.

f. Maintain wholesome and honest Christian **fellowship.**

g. **Beware** counterfeits: *by their fruit you will recognise them* (Mt.7:15,16; Mt.24:24,25).

h. Evaluate your own **"fruit standard"** (without self-condemnatory navel-gazing!) – Gal.5:22,23.

i. Seek and receive **opportunities** for refreshment, retreat, renewal (without "spiritual materialism" of seeking experiences!).

j.*stand firm. Let nothing move you. Always give yourselves fully to the work of the Lord,*..... (1 Cor.15:58).

Christian Unity: Truth and Falsehood

The **substance** of Christian Unity is salvation solely by faith in the Lord Jesus Christ (John 14:6). Christian unity is only **produced** by God the Father, Son and Holy Spirit – not by man (John17:22). Christian disciples and leaders are to **endeavour to maintain** that God-given unity (Eph.4:3); only the Holy Spirit can produce that unity – not us. The **purpose** of Christian unity is to express together loyal, loving teamwork with God to which he calls his disciples towards accomplishing His objectives (1 Cor.3:9).

Unity does not mean uniformity of style. Unity is not to be sought or contrived at any price. Christian unity cannot exist with an admixture of **falsehoods.** Falsehoods are those teachings which either "detract from" or, alternatively, "go beyond" scripture (Rev.22:18-19). Dilutions of truth generate wishful thinking and a works-based hope of heaven. "Going beyond" - increasingly prevalent today - embellishes scripture with false additions/interpretations and teaches self-actualising materialist spiritualities led by self-aggrandising, and frequently profiteering false prophets. These false prophets seek to control the flock of God by "pulling the wool over the eyes" of gullible church leaders, thus infiltrating churches, Christian centres, genuine interdenominational endeavours, ministries and mission (including outreach to the vulnerable – such as the homeless and hungry). Such false prophets must be exposed and stopped. Ezekiel 34 contrasts them with the genuine shepherds who care for God's flock. How can Christian believers identify these false prophets? Some of them are very subtle as Jesus Christ himself warned (Matt.24:24-25); most mix into their presentations apparently legitimate scriptural quotations and parts of great hymns; some are simply hooked/deluded into false teachings which they have flatteringly "been charged" to spread from centres of origin of these falsehoods. Modern media offer false prophets instant easy communication, with superb audio-visual vehicles for their abuse.

The marks/teachings of **falsehoods** which the Bible warns us to avoid, include:

1. Seeking unity based on accepting all that the false prophets teach because they claim "secret knowledge" and rule supreme over us. This is the age-old heresy of **Gnosticism,** which separates "spirituality" from the material and from proper morals.

2. **Prosperity** "gospel": God rewards materially in proportion to self-generated spirituality.

3. That self-generated spirituality can **insulate** from the realities of pain, persecution, suffering, hard work.

4. That one can and should **"move on from the Cross"** and move on from **repentance** into supposed higher echelons of spirituality – one of Satan's most pernicious lies.

5. **Troubles and problems** are wrongly deemed to indicate lack of faith and show poorly self-generated spirituality. Jesus warned of this wrong linkage in the case of the man born blind (John 9:1-3ff).

6. **God cannot do his work without me; together we must dominate/control** *for* **God** – thus the Biblical *dominion covenant* of Gen.1:26-28 which mandates care of creation *under* God becomes arrogant *dominionism* trying to run ahead of God.

7. Followers of falsehoods get **hooked in and held** by false teachers who parade as "gurus" or self-appointed apostles and are reluctant to lose adherents who naïvely give them their adulation and money.

8.   There is an **admixture** of New Age teaching and practices, some hidden to fool many.
9.   Genuine **Christian healing & evangelism** is parodied with instant "assault" methods.

All of the above deny the true nature of the Lord Jesus Christ – who alone appointed the apostles to establish the church originally – including the eleven (Judas Iscariot having betrayed him) plus Matthias his replacement, and Paul the one appointed last *out of time* (1 Cor.15:7-11; 2 Tim.1:1,11). Christian faith rests on Christ's sacrifice for our sins (Rom 3:23), followed by our repentance and continuing life in a state of repentance and faith (1 John 1:7-9), which results in our being forgiven and becoming members of the Church with *Christ in you, the hope of glory* (Col.1:27), urged to emulate the Servant King (Phil.2:5-11) and implement integral mission in His way (1 Cor.3:9).

Figure 7. Contrasts between Biblical Christianity, humanism & the New Age movement

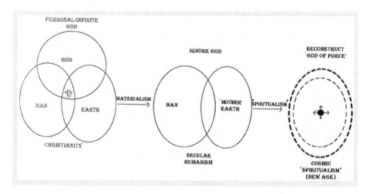

There is a clear distinction between Biblical Christianity that records God coming down to earth in Christ to save us and *religions* that seek by effort to reach upward to God, despite God's great initiative in coming to us for the benefit of **whosoever** will trust him. Christ came ↓ rose from the dead, ascended and will come again, whereas religions strive ↑↑↑.

Suggested Agri-Theology Principles

As an agriculturalist, I was inspired from babyhood by a picture in my bedroom of Jesus as a baby in a manger surrounded by animals - both wild and domesticated - painted by Margaret Tarrant (1888-1959). It carried the text of Psalm 150:6 - *Let everything that has breath praise the LORD. Praise the LORD.* That picture fascinated me from my cot. Later it would inspire me to adopt that text as my mission statement as an agriculturalist. In relation to Integral Mission, it is a challenging text urging stewardship of the conditions in which everything that has breath (all creation - plant, animal and human) can offer praise to the LORD. This is to be done *before* we then praise the LORD ourselves! In 1998, I attended along with 51 others from a total of 26 nations, a workshop in Hohebuch, Germany, on the interface between agriculture and theology. In other words, agri-theology. On the last morning, I awoke at 4 a.m. and penned what follows below as a summary of what emerged from that workshop as I received it.

1.   God is Creator and Sustainer of the universe.
2.   Human beings are created in God's image.
3.   All creation is fallen through sin.
4.   Creation shares in Christ's salvation.
5.   Agriculture is stewardship of creation for food and primary products.
6.   Dominion means authority to manage creation in the way God desires.
7.   The Kingdom of God is both now and future - *creatio continua.*
8.   The Kingdom of God is global and beyond.

9. Perfect relationship is exemplified in the Triune God.
10. People are designed for right relationships: UP (God), OUT (neighbours), DOWN (earth).
11. Only an integrated person will answer for this (Psalm 86:11).
12. Agri-rural Systems need a (w)holistic integrated approach.
13. Farmers are human stewards intended to be in tripartite relationship.
14. Viable rural communities are desirable objectives.
15. Farmers need to be - sensitive to nature; related to land; decisive operators; well-integrated realists; co-operators with God.
16. Rural development needs to provide capacity to:
    - *Care* for creation e.g. Prov.12:10 - know one's beasts;
    - *Share* with those who do not have enough;
    - *Work* in harmony with God (I Cor.3:9);
    - *Be in Place* - relate locally to land and community;
    - *Access Enough* - avoid excessive scale (Isa.5:8).
17. Greed can apply equally to production as to consumption.
18. Christian Ethics are required in agriculture simultaneously to reconcile essentials:- Economy, Ecology, Energy-efficiency, Equity and Employment.
19. Agriculture needs linkage with Christian spirituality.
20. Agriculture is a vocation; Earth is God's farm.

Treasured Nature Thoughts (Lihou Isle, Guernsey 1968)

1.Truth, Beauty and Goodness -
A great panacea?
Or ideals to which
We can seek to adhere?

5. "With God all is possible"
His Word has said -
Why isn't His Book
More frequently read?

2. From concepts to concrete
These ideals change,
When out in God's nature
Our time we arrange.

3. Can rational people
Doubt God in this place,
Far away from the clamour
Of modern rat-race?

4. What then, must these just be
Some fast-fleeting dreams?
Or can we aspire
To live out these themes?

6. For in it you find
The Way, Truth and Life,
If only you'll let Him
Take over your life.

7. Surrender is Victory;
Great peace is known
When we realise we can't
Live ideals on our own

Dominion By Contrast With Dominionism

Dominion refers to one of the God-ordained ways in which he mandates us to relate to his creation in stewardship and caring management (Gen 1:26-28). In addition to this, the Bible instructs us to relate to creation through **companionship** (e.g. Prov.12:10 - know one's beasts), **partnership** (2 Cor.6:1), **teamwork** (1 Cor.12:27-31), and ultimately **priesthood** (in NT times onwards *that of all believers* – 1 Peter 2:9) in order to offer all creation back to God as we care properly through integral mission - Psa.150:6. "Dominion" in the Hebrew language derives from the word *power to crush everything under your feet* (Psalm 8:6-8). Clearly, God does not want us to abuse this power but rather to use it to manage his creation with his guidance and his enabling power to do so by his methods. It is plain for all to see that, through our systemic sin as humans we do not do this faithfully and fully, viz. the global degradation of the natural environment and the neglect and suffering of God's creatures – including weaker humans (such as the unborn, very young and very old). Despite our failings, dominion is our God-given responsibility and we are to pray *your* *kingdom come, your will be done, on earth as it is in heaven* (Matt.6:10) and work loyally towards it. However, it is only God who can restore the earth and establish his Kingdom, which he will do in his time and by his indicated ways when Jesus returns in glory and *every eye shall see him* (Rev.1:7-8). It is not in the gift of man to accelerate or manipulate that return (Acts 1:6-8). God's methods until He returns involve us loyally and humbly serving him, being salt and light (Matt.5:13-16).

Dominionism, by contrast, propounds an Old Testament error by seeking to impose "for God" by worldly ways and warlike power, the imposition of his kingdom – not waiting for God's hour. The people had expected that Jesus would ride into Jerusalem, not on a donkey to die on a cross, but dramatically on a charging warhorse to make them "top nation" with flashes and bangs to impress and silence others. Even after his resurrection, the disciples clung to this vain hope (Acts 1:6) to be told clearly by Jesus that not even he knew the time of his return in glory but that it was in the Father's knowledge and gift alone (Acts 1:7). When He returns, it will be in triumph visible to all (Rev.1:7-8). It is thus a mark of latter-day Gnostic/New Age cults that some propose they can "invoke" the coming of the kingdom and mimic it with fake "signs and wonders" (such as gold dust) seeking the take-over of wealth, power and glory, by infiltrating government (including politics and justice), education, media/arts, families, churches, business and finance (their so-called "Mountains of Influence") and, in short, take control. Such false teaching confuses the gullible and diverts attention from the proper exercise of the gifts of the Holy Spirit (1 Cor. chapters 12 to 14) within characteristic fruit of the Spirit (Gal.5:22,23). This false prophecy of **dominionism** is often accompanied by other aspects of syncretism and cult behaviour, admixing wrong spiritual practices and erroneous teachings (including so-called "going beyond the roadmap of scripture"). One does not need

to look far to find the origins of key dangerous movements seeking
to propagate **dominionism** by gaining control of individuals by false
"transference" and "auto-suggestion" forms of "counselling," and of
families via child manipulation and youth mobilisation – all in the
supposed cause of "evangelism." It is another gospel, another jesus,
another god - (2 Cor.11:13-15; Rev.22:18-19). Faithful shepherds
need to protect the flock against these burgeoning errors with their
seductive music/media, which prove to the discerning that "all that
glitters is not gold;" and to heed the message of Ezekiel 34 & John
10:1-18. **Discernment** is a vital gift in this (1 John 4:1; 1 Cor.12:10;
Heb. 5:14). May God both humble and strengthen us to be his salt and
light in his way until he comes (Mt.5:13-16) standing fast in Christ's
liberty (Gal.5:1)!

CREATIVE FOUNDATIONS

Complexity compels creation; diversity depicts design;
Almightiness affirms assertion,
"Let there be light! And it did shine."
Ideas in minds predate appearance of technologies of man –
Much more the power of our
Creator is displayed and "Yes He can!"

Far above all human striving,
God sets cosmic balance thriving –
Ours the choice to trust, believe, His conceptions to conceive,
Set before us in both Books – Bible truths and Nature looks;
Chain of history to choose God's agenda from His clues –
Biochemical and more, ocean limits on the shore,
Bird migration, feelings fine, intricacies in God's mine
Of wisdom waiting to be tapped,
of praises worthy due unwrapped,
Urgency to care for loss – wonder cast aside as dross,

Fitting facts to theory wild instead of trusting as God's child;
Evolution's hopeless hoax betrays God's own creative hopes.

Chapter 3

Family & Health Matters

Marriage

This is not a matter of opinion, religious or otherwise, but intentionally it is:

1. A monogamous commitment between a man and a woman for companionship and procreation of children based on biological complementarity.
2. For raising the next generation carefully, based on the emotional complementarity of *father and mother* in family units for a sustainable society.
3. **NOT** about rights or lusts but about complementary, co-equal *responsibility* of male and female adults, crucially for unborn children of future generations.

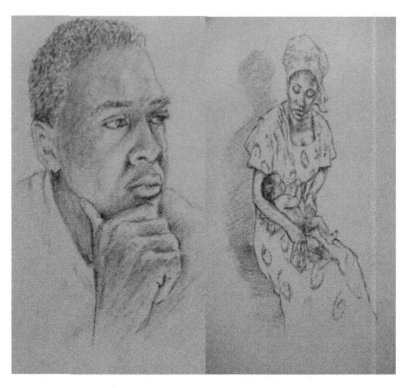

Around the world, the nuclear family unit has provided intergenerational continuity not only of the family line but also of the society as a whole, and the human race. Thus the Bible portrays marriage as a sacred lifelong covenant between a man and a woman as complementary but co-equal partners (Mark 10:6-9; Matt.19:4-6). Bible truth, and biological facts of a 50:50 male: female ratio are arbiters, not human opinion nor human whim.

When asked about divorce, the Lord Jesus Christ explained it was only justified for cases of adultery (Matt.5:31-32; 19:9; Mark 10:2-12; Luke 16:18; 1 Cor.7:10-15). Clearly, in polygamous cultures, discussion of marriage cannot be avoided within integral mission but should be done *extremely* sensitively with love and wisdom. Compassion is wholly appropriate towards those trapped in alternative lifestyles but not affirmation of such lifestyles which are not approved by the Bible (Lev.18:20-24; Romans 1:18-32). In contemporary society, "tolerance" is often hailed as the value above all others but the Bible clearly shows it is not. Potentially and actually, casual tolerance leads to confusion. That confusion is rife wherever there are no *absolutes,* which God gave to all humans for our benefit in the ten commandments (Exod.20:1-17). Governments may counter-legislate against these commandments as some have already done but not without dire and confusing consequences for many people, especially children if they are encouraged to question their God-given identity as either male or female. Jesus spoke very strongly indeed about this (Mark 9:42).

Parenting

The basis of Christian parenting is "training up children in the way they should go" and then claiming the promise of God's Word that *when they are old they will not turn from it* (Prov. 22:6). God has so ordained that this should normally be done by two parents acting as a united team (Rom.15:1-7). Parents are, by definition, stronger than their children in every way initially and are automatic role models for them, even though parents also can learn from their children (Psa.8:2). While Romans 15:1 teaches forbearance with the failings of those weaker, verse 2 enjoins us not to please ourselves. Observation and subsequent life testimony suggest that children are 'pleased' in the long term by being disciplined, by knowing the boundaries of acceptable conduct. Proper discipline not only helps them *relate rightly* within society, with its accepted norms of decency and courtesy, but also towards God with due respect and appreciation of his loving yet Holy Being. A holistic approach is needed towards developing disciples. That process starts with parenting. Being "spiritual" alone is no substitute for maintenance of practical, consistent ground rules of behaviour for children so that they know and respect the boundaries provided. That requires of parents "endurance and encouragement of the Scriptures" so that "we might have hope;" this is God's gift (Rom.15:4,5a). The enjoyment of that endurance and encouragement from God is the fruit – in parenting together as in all relationships – of *the same attitude of mind toward each other that Christ Jesus had, so that with one mind and one voice you may glorify the God and Father of our Lord Jesus Christ.* (Rom.15:5b, 6).

Key rules of *united* parent teamwork are:

1. *Agree together* what the practical rules of behaviour for your children are to be, and
2. *Always support each other in front of them* in carrying them out;
3. Endeavour to *catch children "doing right"* and give appropriate praise.
4. *Be consistent* – do not "flip" from being ultra-affectionate to sudden anger unpredictably
5. *Keep reprimands short* and give assurance of your love while disapproving bad behaviour
6. When you pronounce consequences, be sure to carry them out "if you do that again I'll…"
7. Be angry but don't harbour sin – *do not let the sun go down on your anger* (Eph.4:26)
8. *Review rules privately together;* modify ground rules as children grow up and develop.
9. *Impart & "model" values:* 3 Rs: **Respect** for others; **Responsibility; Restraint** on excess.

There is nothing worse for eroding discipline than when a child is allowed to get away with "playing one parent off against the other" thereby aiming to get what the child wants by devious means. This does not have to be taught; it happens unless parents are vigilant. The good parent is there to say "no" as well as "yes," and both parents need to back one another up in front of their children with utter loyalty (and review later in private discussion if one parent thought the other a little harsh or soft over an issue – NOT challenge the other parent in front of that child, so eroding that parent's authority and respect from the child). Single parents have a tougher time – often as single mothers. In that case, it is important that other adults in the family (grandparents, aunts and uncles) help to share the parenting task. The African proverb says "it takes a village to raise a child." A child must learn to relate in a healthy way to both mother and father role models in their lives. The huge and growing number of orphans or abandoned children pose a massive challenge to the church worldwide, and to specialist ministries to try as far as possible to provide a parenting substitute in as homely an environment as possible.

It is vital that children are given not only a balanced diet for *eating* but also for their *programme; work* (their own chores and helping with real tasks about home, compound and farm or business), *rest* for reflection and learning to "be still," and *play* in which real fun is had as well as learning to share with other children. Children brought up in multi-child families need each parent to give some individual attention to each one every day, while an "only child" needs regular socialising with other children to learn to "rough and tumble," to share toys and to share the time of adult attention. Secure, well-integrated children have regular *praise* (**without** bribes for good conduct), regular *reprimands* (**without** parental recriminations or "nagging") and are set *timed goals* (not just "do that *now*" but "do that by the count of ten"). Good parents teach children Eph.6:1-3 and then practice verse 4 *do not exasperate your children.* While "acute provocation" (most notoriously by parents who lose their tempers with children) is the more obvious way of exasperating anyone, perhaps the more insidious way of exasperating one's children is NOT to keep to **boundaries,** NOT to maintain **discipline.** Parents lay the foundation for lifelong *discipleship* in Christ. It is a solemn and crucial role to be done with a blend of prayerfulness and pragmatism.

Children At Risk

In poorer communities of Africa and elsewhere, children are at particular risk as well as among richer but dysfunctional or undisciplined families. Children are highly vulnerable to the internet and what it peddles from pornography, to violence, to paedophile-grooming, to drug-dealing. Not only so, but unscrupulous parents desperate for some means of income even sell their own children with many ending up as exploited labour or within the ugly sex trade. Integral mission must include children or it is not worthy of its name! Of course, full children's work involves specialisms that not every integral mission organisation possesses. However, the agenda of any integral mission venture can and should include:-

a.   advocacy for children;
b.   facilities and school curricula including ample play;
c.   nurturing their sense of wonder in God's creation;
d.   training church leaders in child-friendly worship/teaching provision within churches;
e.   parenting training within marriage preparation classes;
f.   engaging communities in awareness of child justice and welfare issues;
g.   points to consider in making risk assessments for child protection;
h.   Bible education for all ages of young people, up to leaving for higher education.

In many countries now, all organisations are required to conduct "fitness" screening of workers who wish to minister among children – and other vulnerable groups of people. Very sadly, there have been far too many cases of child abuse – emotional, mental or physical – within the church and avowedly Christian organisations. Increasingly, governments operate systems of disclosure of any criminal records that would bar a person from future work with children for the protection not only of children themselves but also of organisations seeking to provide properly Biblical standards of child care. Wise specialist children's ministries carry out full risk assessments of their premises and procedures to ensure child-safe provision. Jesus spoke very strongly of those who harm children in any way,

> *If anyone causes one of these little ones who believe in Me to sin, it would be better for him to be thrown into the sea with a large millstone tied around his neck.*
>
> —Mark 9:42; Mt.18:6; Lk.17:2

As Proverbs 22:6 teaches: *Start children off on the way they should go, and even when they are old they will not turn from it.* Notably, Jesus rebuked His disciples for turning away young children, saying *Let the little children come to me, and do not hinder them, for the kingdom of God belongs to such as these* (Mark10:14; Mt.19:14; Lk.18:15-17).

It has been said that "God has no grandchildren, only children" to indicate that the Christian faith is not inherited. Each generation, each individual, has to decide whether or not to follow Jesus Christ as their Saviour and Lord. How they are taught and cared for in childhood can make it more or less likely that they will choose early to commit their lives into his unfailing care. They need to learn that integral mission concerns every aspect of life now and eternally.

Child Protection

'Children' means babies, toddlers, infants and youngsters up to the age of 16. In some countries, the legal definition of "children" may include up to 18 years old as being the minimum age when they can marry, and vote in elections. Generally, the smaller or younger the child, the greater the need for protection. The growing practice of aborting unwanted embryos and babies for convenience or "face-saving" of the parents is deplorable; actually, it is murder except in very specific and rare situations. Bullying is usually considered only to apply to abuse of smaller children by bigger ones but what of adults who wilfully abandon/abort babies simply for their own convenience? Thus, advocacy is needed for protection to include unborn children, and against child prostitution/ trafficking. Biologically, a new being in

God's image begins at conception ready to implant her/himself in the uterus.

Protection includes not only the more obvious shielding of children from physical harm and extreme poverty but also their protection from mental, emotional and spiritual abuse (including brainwashing). The best context for protection that a child can have is from its two parents humbly depending upon God as its creator. Such parents need to rely upon God to help them to train up that child in the way to go through life so that when old that child will not depart from those correct precepts (Proverbs 22:6). This requires parents to accept responsibility to provide for their child:- security, discipline, correction, "tough love," constructive criticism and regular praise and encouragement when the child does right [see section on Parenting above]. Of course, tragically, many children do not have such parents. Some do not know their father, others are abandoned by both parents, while many are orphaned by the early death of their parents. In these cases, the extended family or the church or civil society may assume responsibility for those needy children.

Children are at risk from their environment, from other badly-behaved children and from unscrupulous adults. There is a balance to be struck between harmful exposure of children at one extreme and soft "cushioning" of them from life's realities at the other such that they are unprepared for adult life. For instance, proper training of children should include responsible adults allowing and enabling them to encounter normal challenges of life in the form of tough experiences, such as battling against harsh weather, playing tough sports and helping others when it may be less than comfortable for them to do so. "Spoilt" children who "almost always get their own way" are universally unpopular in all cultures and unless redeemed from their "overprotected" background, generally become selfish, underachieving adults. However, there are ever-intensifying threats to children in today's electronically interconnected world. Through films and other media and via their peers, they become aware quickly of such evils as violence, sexual promiscuity, deviant self-harming behaviours, harmful drugs and their abuse, and attitudes of greed, materialism and casual or wasteful treatment of both other people and resources. Protection from wrong values is vital. As in medicine, the best protection is preventative. Children need role models to impart the right attitudes, behaviours and goals within God-given boundaries - notably as taught in the Bible - towards lifestyle, proper sexual behaviour, and rightly relating to other people and to world resources.

Due legislation is required for those who work with children to be checked for their criminal records since sadly too many have abused the privilege of their contact with children to mistreat them sexually or in other bad ways. Child protection includes such precautions. Jesus took a child to illustrate that we should welcome such little ones in his name, and in so doing welcome him and God the Father too (Mark 9:36,37). This mirrors the protection God so longs to give all his children who trust him (Psalm 91).

Positive Christian parenting needs to be taught and there is a need for advocacy for children's welfare and protection. Specific children's ministries - such as sequential child education by age group - may require specialist ministries with trained leaders and managers. However, child integration into families and communities based on due child care should be taught within wholistic development.

Youth

"Youth" can cover a range of ages from older children (over 10) to young adults (up to 20-25). In any case, people mature at different rates and some conditions leave people at a younger developmental stage than their chronological age. In Africa, average life expectancy is often low by European standards so that the average age of those in church leadership and other responsible positions is relatively lower. Pitt was Prime Minister of Britain aged 24; music composer Mozart died aged 35. However, whatever definition of "youth" is chosen, some missions historically do not target youth work *per se* as the mission focus. Nevertheless, youth work is a key part of integral mission as it is designed to enable younger as well as older people. Many training approaches are predominantly through participatory, informal, adult educational methods including extension via groups. However, young people should be brought into such groups as soon as possible; some at 11 or 12 are working hard and motivated to do such things as grow their own vegetables to pay their own school fees. Many young adults are alumni of such welcoming courses. Integral Mission service is for wholistic development through Christian churches and churches consist of all ages! Young people are not only "potential" and "seed corn of the future church" but also key members of the church *now* on the same grounds of grace as other believers; they have actual opinions, ideas and unique abilities to offer *now*. Youth are actors in integral mission, not just passive recipients/beneficiaries of it. Young people learn by doing and the healthy church will risk asking them to *participate* rather than just running a youth ministry *for* them. God speaks through young people to older ones (e.g. Psalm 8:2; 1 Sam.3:1-21; Matt.18:1-5). Some young people in churches are, of course, yet to put their trust in the Lord Jesus Christ and "God has no grandchildren" such that each generation must choose whether or not to follow Christ for themselves. Sharing the steps to such faith must always be a key part of work among young people.

Integral Mission agencies need to develop disciples in their own teams and through their regular work. However, there are particular pressures for young people in changing from children into adults biologically, psychologically and socially, which can be recognised worldwide. Peer pressure is particularly acute among teenagers and there is often a tension between the desire to conform to group norms and the equally strong wish to rebel and be different, especially against authority figures. This is a normal part of the transition from dependence as a small child through to independence as an adult and integration as a mature member of society. Teenagers often express in various ways that they feel insecure during this transition using terms like "ugly, unloved and useless." Their reaction to feeling "ugly," however irrational that may seem, may manifest itself in an obsession with their appearance and to "posing" by some in counteraction. Their reaction to feeling "unloved" can be to seek and be vulnerable to "love in the wrong places," such as in various forms of illicit sexual activity. Their reaction to feeling "useless" can be to strive neurotically to make their mark and to become overwhelmed by anxiety that they can never be good enough, leading some to the despair of suicide, which is all too common among actually multi-talented young people.

We need to incorporate an understanding of these issues within counselling work and training. Particular attention needs to be paid to the burgeoning issue of HIV/AIDS, which is especially likely to start among the young and to become a scourge within a shortened life thereafter. HIV/AIDS work should not be a 'specialised ministry' alone but should be part of integral mission along with peer education and offering alternative lifestyles and livelihood skills (see section on HIV/AIDS). Healthy discussion is needed of issues of sexual behaviour, alcohol, drugs, smoking and other temptations openly in homes, churches, and communities. Open evening meetings under the stars where all can hear and then question and discuss are particularly healthy if well conducted and led with Biblical principles for life, relationships and marriage, exhorting youths to *remember your Creator in the days of your youth* (Eccl.12:1). Relationships with young people built early on in their lives stand the test of the potentially stormy teenage years. Contrary to the saying of the Victorian era, children are to be seen and heard, listened to and trained up from a young age (Prov. 22:6).

HIV/Aids & Related Matters

HIV = Human Immunodeficiency Virus, is the cause of AIDS = Acquired Immune Deficiency Syndrome in which lymphocytes (white blood cells) are destroyed thus causing loss of the body's ability to protect itself against disease. AIDS is transmitted by sexual intercourse, through infected blood and blood products, and to the unborn child via the placenta. HIV/AIDS is neither contracted by shaking hands with someone already infected nor by sitting on a seat on which they have sat. It first came to recognition in Rakai District, SW Uganda.

HIV/AIDS can be contracted innocently by unborn children, through blood transfusions with infected blood, and within normal sexual relationships in marriage where one of the couple has been previously infected. Infection is particularly spread through promiscuous sexual relationships (both heterosexual and homosexual) which account for much of its rise to prominence, together with the use of infected needles for injections – especially among drug addicts. Propensity to contract HIV/AIDS is thus greatest among sexually active but undisciplined young people and where there is a lack of gainful activity in work, home life and recreation. Poverty tends to exacerbate the incidence of HIV/AIDS and to increase the chances of its spread in a community where there are shortages - physical, moral and spiritual.

Compassion and care are appropriate towards those who have HIV/AIDS, no matter how they came to get it. This must be clearly distinguished from approval of the lax sexual behaviour which predisposes people and communities to get HIV/AIDS. Care may include the provision of anti-retro-viral treatment at as reasonable a cost as possible, as well as eventual hospice care. God cares for orphans and widows (Psa. 68:5; Hosea 14:3) many of whom are the result of HIV/AIDS.

Teaching on the facts about HIV/AIDS and the means of prevention is vital within all holistic development education. Tackling the need for Biblical understanding, discipleship development, sustainable livelihoods, gainful employment and skills training should underpin all efforts to combat HIV/AIDS. The use of peer educators (e.g. among young people) in society can help greatly in the effort against HIV/AIDS where those peer educators practice what they preach. Some may have been delivered from lax lifestyles and still have

HIV/AIDS but have a Christian testimony to their deliverance and now act as a warning to others.

The Bible teaches that the joy and fulfilment of proper sexual relations should occur only within marriage. Pre-marital sexual intercourse is not appropriate, nor are sexual relations between those of the same sex, nor with animals (Lev.18:20-24; Romans 1:18-32). Faithfulness within marriage is vital, not only to avoid the risk of HIV/AIDS but also in itself as a norm of God's ordinances for human behaviour (Luke 16:18; Hebrews 13:4). It is, therefore, appropriate to abstain from sexual relations except within marriage. The use of condoms is a legitimate means of preventing unwanted pregnancies within marriage. Condoms also can help protect a married person from an unfaithful spouse. However, condoms are not 100% effective in preventing either pregnancy or the possibility of HIV/AIDS infection. Condoms should not be advocated simply to enable a sexually promiscuous lifestyle.

Discipleship development, together with addressing the conditions for gaining sustainable livelihoods are the priorities in addressing HIV/AIDS and HIV/AIDS programmes need to be offered in this context and not as stand-alone ministries.

Health

"Health" carries the meaning of both "wholeness" and "holiness." A "wholistic" approach to health implies integral well-being of individuals spiritually and mentally as well as physically, emotionally and socially. It springs from right relationships both intra-personally and inter-personally, as well as with God and with the rest of creation. The word "health" relates to an Old English word [*hael, haelig* = whole, holy] now spelt "hale" as in "hale and hearty" - meaning "vigorous."

"Health" not only describes a state of absence of disease but rather positively denotes a state of comprehensive well-being. In this fallen world, health is compromised and suffering results, sometimes by our directly sinful behaviour but also owing to the generally dysfunctional state of the world by contrast with its God-designed wholeness (Gen.1:31; Gen.2:9 cf. Gen.3:17-19).

The message and hope of scripture is for ultimate *shalom* (God's all-encompassing peace; Zech.14:9; 1 Thess.5:23). One of the compound names of God in the Bible is *Jehovah-rapha (ropheca)* = The LORD our Healer or Health (Exod.15:26; Psa.23:3).

Health may be considered to include:- absence of disease (Deut.7:15); healing (Matt.8:2,3); sound health (Luke 5:31); well-being (Acts 27:34); sound doctrine (3 John 2); deliverance (Psa.42:11); wound healing (Jer.30:17); harmony (Prov.16:24). When there is a breakdown of health, it is not for us to apportion blame (John 9:1-3) but rather to seek to alleviate suffering.

Encouraging service to bring wholeness to others (as in Isa.58:6-14) may include:

- promotion of awareness of the interconnectedness of total lifestyle and health
- the link between water quality, nutrition, sanitation, hygiene and health
- importance of prophylaxis / prevention of disease rather than just curative treatment
- role of prayer for healing and the promotion of the healing ministry in churches
- priority of primary health care at the community level
- growing scourge of HIV/AIDS, its prevention and compassionate treatment

- alleviation of poverty which predisposes communities to greater risks of ill-health
- links between stress and health, and the growing incidence of stress-causing factors
- enabling the strategies of health-oriented organisations e.g. *The Leprosy Mission*
- addressing particular health needs through specialists in our team e.g. eye clinics
- promotion of natural medicines (see www.anamed.org and the work of REAP)

Health is a matter of God's sovereignty, not for human demand as a right but rather for nurture by treating our bodies as temples of the Holy Spirit (1 Cor.6:19-20) and respecting others likewise. Advocacy is needed on wider environmental and social issues affecting health such as global climate change, land degradation, land-grabbing, livelihood sustainability & gratuitous portrayal of violence, greed, raw evil & promiscuity in the media.

Coping With Loss–Bereavement, Brokenness, Disappointment

The Bible has much to say about lament, especially in the Psalms where the writers are very open and honest with God and with their fellow humans. Of course, the Book of Lamentations is there yet relatively seldom preached. However, the reality of life, especially among the poor and marginalised, consists of frequent and sometimes sustained losses. In many places, miscarriages are common, and sometimes are deliberately induced, which the Bible calls murder. Some estimates reckon that the average rate of miscarriage may be as high as 1 in 4 pregnancies. Certainly, infant mortality is very high in some countries with levels of 6 to 7% recorded. Of course, all of us lose relatives and friends and suffer bereavements all the time. While the Bible offers much about coping with this, do we offer enough through our integral mission work? I suspect not. In too many churches, the "church culture" might be summed up as "praise the Lord anyway." In a way, this expresses the abiding praiseworthiness of God whatever our own personal or community circumstances, yet it denies the reality of suffering. Paul urges (Romans (12:15) *Rejoice with those who rejoice; mourn with those who mourn.* We cannot know how someone else feels and are unwise to say we do! However, we can empathise, that is try to put ourselves in their circumstances and seek to imagine how we might feel. Frequently, this may simply mean sitting with them in silence – a common feature of some rural African cultures.

Loss of people and possessions may come through conflict between warring clans, through theft, or fire, or floods, famine or pestilence. Loss may take the form of disappointed hopes – a job not given to us, a harvest that was smaller than we wished. Health may falter and we may lose, and will lose as we age, some of our former physical vigour, and perhaps mental vigour as well. The good news is that we may grow spiritually all our days by God's grace if we seek him. As David says, *I was young and now I am old, yet I have never seen the righteous forsaken or their children begging bread.* (Psa.37:25).

As we sustain losses and yet prove God's faithfulness through them we grow through broken-ness, as Job famously did when he never lost faith in the sovereign goodness of God, despite even his own wife's urging him to give up and curse God. Broken-ness is characteristic of a true disciple of Christ. That is to say, readiness to "turn the other cheek" when attacked physically, or more usually perhaps, verbally. Broken-ness allows others to be preferred before us. An attitude of broken-ness enables us to humble ourselves, to put others ahead of ourselves, to display the fruit of the Spirit (Gal.5:22-23). Supremely, Jesus showed this quality of humility and broken-ness as Paul expressed it so well in Phil.2:1-11 culminating in his death for us on the Cross.

In all this, we do well to remember that Jesus Christ is King of Kings and Lord of Lords. Perhaps one of the best reminders of this truth is the lion who is King of the Savannah!

Chapter 4

Church Matters

Transformational Development Lessons from Nehemiah

The Book of Nehemiah (c. BC 446-434) in the Old Testament follows that of his contemporary, the priest Ezra. Together they worked in integral mission among the people of God to restore the broken walls of Jerusalem. Many lessons for churches today can be learned as a prelude to reviewing their own integral mission work in stewardship of the gospel of Christ.[NB Nehemiah chapters 8 to 12 contain material also reported in the book of Ezra; these chapters may have been written by Ezra, since they are in the second person]. A brief overview of Nehemiah follows. He was cup-bearer (very trusted role of butler) in Sushan (Susa, in Iran) to the Emperor Artaxerxes, perhaps the most powerful ruler on earth at the time. Nehemiah heard bad news from his native Jerusalem that its walls were in ruins. He was sorely distressed. The king observed this and asked about it. Nehemiah used the opportunity to ask for travel documents to return to Jerusalem where he instigated rebuilding the walls, organising teams as Governor and working with Ezra to reinstate the worship of the LORD God.

Overview of the Book of Nehemiah and Questionsfor Churches today

Chapter 1

Bad news of home (vv.1-4) and prayerful reactions to it (vv. 5-11). *Questions on 1.* How do we receive news of reality, and how do we respond to it? What can we learn from Nehemiah?

Chapter 2

Honest-faced behaviour (vv.1-4) and planned prayerful requests (vv.5-9). Opposition registered (v.10). Systematic survey (vv. 11-16), motivation of people (vv.17-18), and gainsayers resisted (vv. 19-20). *Questions on 2.* Do we hide our real feelings unhelpfully? Are we prepared with the right requests when opportunity presents itself? Do we mobilise teams? Are we vigilant and firm against opposition?

Chapter 3

Delegation of duties in accomplishing the task. *Question on 3.* Are we using all those we have in a planned, comprehensive way for God's glory?

Chapter 4

Opposition – subtle and persistent (vv.1-3) but triumph in the face of it (vv.4-6). Though ongoing plotting against them (vv.7-8) but victory by prayer and work with guardianship (vv.9-23, including trumpeters, and workers with trowels and spears). *Questions on 4.* Are we ready for challenges to God's way? Are we aware of spiritual warfare?

Chapter 5

Opposition from within (vv.1-5). Nehemiah averts a strike and institutes justice among the workers (vv.6-13), forgoing his personal allowance (vv.14-19).

Questions on 5. How might we ensure committed, joyful teamwork? How deal with problems?

Chapter 6

Opposition renewed and intensified, with persistent attempts to distract, intimidate and falsify (vv.1-14). Completion of the wall despite all this opposition (vv.15-19).

Questions on 6. Are we alert to the many subtle as well as overt stratagems of Satan against God's church? What counter measures are to be used?

Chapter 7

Keep a watch (v.3) and a register (v.5) of all the people and their resources.

Questions on 7. Do we know our people and have we developed a means of mobilising those able to help as well as caring for those in need?

Chapter 8

God's Word openly declared (vv.1-5) leads to joy (v.6) and understanding (vv.7-8) and sharing with the needy (v.10). The whole church was joyful (v.12) and the people impacted their civil society and reinstated the Festival of Booths (temporary shelters) – vv.14-18.

Questions on 8. Are we so declaring and applying the Word of God to the whole of our lives that the church is joyful and impacting the whole of our community? How could we do it better?

Chapter 9
There is time management (v.3), corporate worship of the God of history (vv.5-31) and application to their current situation then.

Questions on 9. What warning about prosperity is in verses 25-31? What application is made to their current situation in verses 32-38?

Chapter 10
There is a need to make a covenant with God (vv.1-30) and so restore right stewardship (v.31) to achieve an economic outcome (vv.35-37) with the priests also included in tithing to God (v.38).

Questions on 10. What are the incomes and livelihoods in our place like? Do they reflect right stewardship? If not, why not? What can we do about it according to this chapter?

Chapter 11
Correct and shared oversight of the congregation, with each person using their particular talents (vv.12, 14, 16, 17, 19, 22) then there is outreach to the surrounding villages (vv.25 ff.).

Questions on 11. What changes to church management do you need to make in order to have every person using their talents, and so to reach out into your community?

Chapter 12
When church leaders relate well to each other there is building up of the community with thanksgiving (vv.27, 31) and there is church order with resources given to enable the ministry (v.44) with praise resulting (v.46). Obedience leads to ample resources being released for the work of God and consequent genuine praise.

Questions on 12. How well are we relating to each other as church leaders and church members? Does the society around know more about our divisions than about Jesus who unites us?

Chapter 13

When we relax and think we have arrived, beware those people and attitudes coming in which are not of God (v.6), which lead to lack of tithing (v.10), neglect of the Sabbath (vv.15-18) and sexual misbehaviour (vv.23-27).

Questions on 13. What does this chapter of Nehemiah's book show about the ongoing need for a transformational gospel with integral mission, and for Christian stewardship reviews?

Parish and Congregation Development

Development is measured by improvement in quality of church life, ministry and integral mission. In order to focus vision for this and to mobilise a parish or congregation towards achieving it together, a review process is recommended. This is equivalent to a properly-run "family meeting," designed to be frank but friendly!

Principles

1. The church is an **international family business** with local branches of co-workers.
2. The purpose of the church is to glorify God by **building his Kingdom as a team.**
3. The Kingdom is built by being, doing and sharing through **prayer, planning and practice.**
4. Motivation for Kingdom-building is through **relationships** (of respect and of responsible companionship) - with God, with each other and with the rest of creation.
5. We have the authority (dominion) to offer **what God likes** in good stewardship together.
6. Jesus alluded to having the right relationship towards **material** possessions in some 40% of his recorded teachings.

7.   What is required is *caring resource management* **to enable the vision, ministries within and mission beyond the church using our talents, time and money to achieve it.** It is vital that each person finds their role, their gifting and pursues that – those to farm, farm well; those to start other businesses, to do so with vigour; those to lead in the home, in the church, or to serve in all sorts of ways to do so with the sense of calling (vocation) God wishes each person to have as they live as disciples of Jesus Christ.

This approach has been found to work in practice in Africa, UK and elsewhere, in parishes large and small, rural and urban, theologically "high" and "low." Typical samples measured have yielded the order of 35%+ increase in volunteering with 35%+ increase in financial giving (depending upon the base level at the outset).

Procedures

1.   The church council needs to appoint a **planning group** to oversee the review process. This should consist of some 7 or 8 people, ideally only half being from among the church council members and with the Pastor, Vicar or Rector as Chaplain to the Group (NOT its Chairman).

2.   The planning group needs to begin by meeting together to pray over the whole process. An overview of the Book of Nehemiah makes a suitable stimulus for this since it draws timeless lessons for collaborative development in God's Kingdom work.

3.   The planning group needs to compile, using the skills of those within the parish, a **prayer card or spoken message** for distribution to undergird the whole review process.

4.   All those with an interest in the development of the parish/ congregation concerned should be invited (with a recorded reply system of some sort) to a **review day.**

5.   There needs to be follow-up with a parish plan written stating "what we offer now;" "what we would like to offer;" and "how and when we hope to achieve it." Volunteers can then be invited to commit time, talents and money to enable the implementation of the plan. Progress occurs when people and possessions are mobilised towards such a vision for parish development. The parish plan can then be reviewed annually and rewritten after say five years. In this way, a church can monitor its "health" in terms of its integral mission activity.

Churches & Conflict Resolution

There are recognised steps within this important process:

- Identify sources of conflict:- greed; scarcity; lust; power; pride; status (Prov.6:16-19).
- Consider sites of conflict:- self (Jer. 17:9; Mark 7:20-23; Jas.4:1-5; Rom.7:18-19); family (Gen.37:28); community (Lev.19:13-18); nations (Psa.2:1-4).
- Solutions for conflict:
  - Be angry but do not sin; don't let the sun go down on your wrath (Eph.4:26);
  - Name, shame, repent [= admit, back down, confess] 2 Chron.7:14
  - Desire forgiveness; endeavour to forget; let go and let God;
  - New heart (Ezek.36:26); shalom Isa.2:2-4; submit (Jas.4:6-10);
  - Endeavour to maintain the unity of the Spirit (Eph.4:3); Rom.8.

- Civil reformation:- Nehemiah; we have a transforming gospel for **peace-building:**
- Peace Prescription: Eph.2:12-22, esp. v.14; James 3 – control your tongue and be wise
- Peace Process: Zech.9:10
- Peace Promises: Isa.32:13-20; John 14:27; Matt.5:9; Phil.4:1-9
- **Reconciliation** = *katallage 'exchange' (katallasso; apokatallasso; diakatallasso)*
- Reconciliation means "restored relationships;" The Cross symbolises all four of these relationships (God, self, neighbours, earth)
- Reconciliation is the basis for sustainable conflict resolution;
- It is interpersonal, intercommunal and springs especially from awareness of one's own sin
- Follows only from truth, justice and forgiveness (Christian imperatives in civil society)
- Links with atonement through the blood of Jesus on the cross; justification by faith
- It is enabled powerfully when we are deeply conscious of our need for God's forgiveness
- Full reconciliation is a sovereign work of God the Father, Son and Holy Spirit.
- Reconciliation needs **VIM** (Venter, 2004): "Vision of what you want to become; Intention to act; Means to do it;"
- Venter (2004) lists:- Exposure/storytelling; relationship and reality; value of each soul and of restoring justice in the practical reconciliation process;
- Develop friendships, groups; mutual storytelling, teaching, services and acts of restitution, trips, teamwork;

- "Advocacy for/doing of reconciliation is a prerequisite for sustainable community development" ...
- OT cases: Gen.3-4; Gen.25-33; Gen.37,42-45; Josh.22; 2 Sam 11-12, Psa.51; I Kings 21
- Gospel cases: Mt.5:21-26; 6:12; 18:15-35; Lk.10:30-36; 15:11-32; Lk.19:1-10; Jn.1:4-42
- Other NT cases: Acts 6:1-7; 9:1-31; 10; Gal.2:11-16; Gal.3:26-29; Eph.2:11-22; 2 Cor.5:16-21; Philemon.
- Justice follows true righteousness (vertical relationship to God results in horizontal restitutions towards neighbours and earth!)
- Justice, peace and the integrity of Creation hang together in wholistic development.

Strategic Management at Congregation Level

It is important for congregations to carry out periodic *Christian Stewardship Reviews for Parish Development* (please see section above). However, there are several strategies that can benefit the management of parish affairs in more Biblical ways than those often pursued through pressure of events and lack of time taken out for strategic thinking. Below are outlined some of the measures which might profitably be considered.

The Pastor as "bottleneck"

The term "bottleneck" here does not carry any reference to the collar worn by pastors. Rather, it refers to the fact that they often become unduly stressed by having all messages and issues of congregational and parish life passing through their desks and now often through their mobile telephones and computers. In the Old Testament, Moses was advised by his father-in-law Jethro to take due rest and to delegate responsibilities because he was heading towards "burn-out"

(Ex.18:17-24). "Helps" and "administrations" are listed as gifts to the church (1 Cor.12:27,28); all the body parts need to be mobilised. Practical progress in relation to this matter may include the following:

1. Teaching the Biblical principles of 'Body' ministry and working out their application to current church management issues.
2. Setting up a church administration office with free-standing telephone, using the existing clerk and a guard – who could both be church members, part voluntary and part supported from congregational love gifts.
3. In the absence of means to set up No.2 straightaway, an interim measure might be to identify one or more church members to whose mobile telephones calls may be diverted one day per week so that the pastor's day off is not cluttered with telephone messages and e-mails to deal with.
4. Setting up groups under the chairmanship of members other than the pastor – but with the pastor as chaplain to those groups, so that responsibility and leadership skills are shared and developed within the Body.

The Church site as Information point

Developing the church site as an extension education point can enhance its testimony, widen its contacts with the community and its needs, and make better use of its unique and strategic position in the civil society, better reflecting its integral mission. Ways of implementing this might include:

1. Planting and labelling useful trees – such as *Moringa oleifera, Tephrosia, Leucaena, Bamboo* – with an outline of their multiple uses.
2. Clearing any litter so that the church site is clean and tidy.

3. Providing (at the church office) a village notice board for messages and for useful posters about farming, household, livelihood, health, and church outreach issues.

4. Starting a village Reading Room at the church office, or in an open-sided rest hut where leaflets (both evangelistic and developmental) might be kept.

5. Considering setting up a village dam or other water resource point at the church site. For instance, the church may provide a treadle pump and siphoning system and have several vegetable gardens which could be competitively managed by different younger members of the congregation, using good practices such as composting and mulching. Prizes might be given each season for the best results and a proportion of each grower's produce (10% perhaps) given out to the elderly, needy widows, or those disabled in some way, as a visible sign of the church's caring role in society.

6. Daring sensitively to use the church as a venue to discuss openly (on a community basis) the impacts of some cultural traditions which damage the nation – such as widow-cleansing (linked to HIV/AIDS etc.), forcible retrieval of property from widows by in-laws (acting as outlaws in terms of Biblical ethics!), elaborately costly funerals (which debilitate survivors & deny the reality of Christian views of heaven).

Chapter 5

Environment Considerations

God's Commitment to the Natural World

Commitment concerns relationships rather than mechanisms, the what and why of creation rather than the how and when. It is about God's celebration, care and compassion towards his creation rather than a review of human attempts to rationalise its mysteries and wonders. Suffice to say that for the author, the case for creation as per the Bible accounts rather than evolution is overwhelming, and complexity compels creation. Here are explored some of the key Biblical texts that provide insights into God's commitment to the natural world, which he created and creates. God's glory is revealed by his Spirit, not only through the Bible but also through the natural world. It concludes by summarising some implications for human responses arising from the revelation of God's motivation towards the natural world.

1. *Who is this? – even the wind and the waves obey him!* – Mark 4:41
2. *In the beginning, God created…* - Genesis 1:1
3. *The earth is the LORD's and everything in it…* – Psa.24:1
4. *God saw that it was good* – recurring phrase of Gen.1

5. Gen.1 : **Time & Things** – teamwork in creation by The Holy Trinity

6. Gen.2 : **Place & Purpose** rest, provision, care, relationship; tree beautiful/useful (v.9)

7. Gen.3 : **Doubt & Death** fall & consequences (Rom.8:19ff); seeds of salvation (3:15)

8. Job 38 & 39, who? (38:4); beauty "peacocks" (39:13); utility "horsepower" (39:19-25)

9. Psalmists' recognition of God's commitment Psa 8; Psa 104; Psa 150

10. Prophet's recognition of human degradation of environment and creatures – Hosea 4:1-3

11. Bread, manna, "companionship," Shepherding – Psa 23; Ezekiel 34

12. Chronicles: recognition of links:- creation, repentance, salvation, land (2 Chron.7:14).

False Dichotomies are often presented between the following:

Material v. spiritual; theology v. geography (place context; Micah 4:4); now v. later (time context – neither procrastination nor panic action); faith v. works; man v. nature; church v. world (the church is to be in the world but not of it); contemplation, reflection, silence v. words, reasoning, song; Word v. Spirit (they always combine in genuine Biblical practice).

Let us remember, as stated earlier, that integrity in the Cross symbolises the whole Gospel as it points UP to God, OUT to neighbours, and DOWN to earth.

Integrity Intent in Our Relationships to Earth &Its Creatures

The following are all important ways in which we are to relate to creation:

1. **Dominion** = "complete authority" - to do *what God likes* with creation, not to dominate it! (Gen. 1:26-28) – so **Lead.**
2. **Priesthood** = the role to let creation express itself in praise to God (Psalm 150:6) and to offer it to God with praise – so **Offer.**
3. **Companionship** = respectful relationship with creatures (Prov.12:10) – so **Befriend.**
4. **Stewardship** = accountable, caring management of resources (Luke 16:2) - so **Manage.**
5. **Teamwork** = co-worker in a team effort, with God (1 Cor.3:9) as modelled by The Trinity – so **Partner.**

Creation & harmony are embedded within its: rhythms & cycles; activity & rest (Mark 6:31); seasons & seasonality (Gen.8:22; Eccl.3:1).

Justice, peace & the integrity of creation is found in: Isa.61:11; **in Christ** (Col.1:15-23; John 11:35). There are boundaries to be observed if we are to seek God's blessing:

BOUNDARIES FOR BLESSING

O God of all our boundaries, of landmarks tried and true
We bow in humble access through Christ Our Lord to You.
When we transgress those
boundaries, grow consequential weeds
And many are the sufferers of such ill-placed misdeeds.

We ask Your blessing King of
Kings – our sovereign Nation bleeds

As we behold sad outcomes of materialistic creeds.
Help us recover Your good sense
to mend each broken bound'ry fence –
The fence round species, farm
and life, our nationhood's defence

From BSE * to FMD, far distant errors strike
The heart of rural livelihoods, on vale and hill and dyke.
Eternal values beckon yet and
hope's clear beacon seals our debt
To You Our Father; please forgive when we ourselves forget.

When we forget You own each
cow on thousand hills around,
Where You, Great Shepherd, tread
and love each spot of sacred ground,
And You each seed make to
abound, give ev'ry animal its sound…
We offer You time, talents, skills; our
hearts, our minds and stubborn wills;
Great Mender of earth's many
spills, grant us a blessing that fulfils.

*Penned by the author during Foot-
and-Mouth Disease FMD in the UK, 2001*
* BSE = Bovine Spongiform Encephalopathy

Environment Matters

Biblical understanding of the environment proposes teaching and
action for our relationships as fellow creatures of God the Creator in
his provided, shared habitat of the earth for the benefit of all creation
(*oikonomia* – which means "laws/rules of management for home").

1.   God created. *In the beginning God created the heavens and the earth* (Genesis 1:1), as a pure act of his will, out of nothing, each "after its kind" and he continuously sustains it. God reminded Job of this (Job 38:5-11).

2.   God placed man in the garden of Eden to *tend and guard and keep it* (Gen.2:15, Amplified Bible), with just one prohibition (not to eat of the tree of the knowledge of good and of evil, Gen.2:17) but including the privilege of naming the creatures (Gen.2:19). The human context within creation is well expressed by Psalm 8.

3.   Creation is made both beautiful and useful (Gen.3:5; Isaiah 41:19,20). Human neglect of proper creation care (defiance of the Gen.2:17 prohibition) led to the fall of all creation and ignoring the warnings of Deuteronomy 8:6-20 led to its dysfunctional state of "groaning" (Jeremiah 12:4,11; Romans 8:22). Our failure to serve as loyal co-operators under God, not observing his ten commandments, results in dire environmental consequences as noted by the prophet Hosea 4:1-3.

4.   God's agenda, to be signalled by the return of the Lord Jesus Christ to earth (mentioned in the Bible some 300 times) is to renew heaven and earth (Revelation 21:1). However, until then, he has not revoked his charge to us to relate rightly to this present one (Psalm 115:16) as His tenants, **not** owners. Right relationship to earth and its creatures arises from right relationship to God (Mark 12:30) and to each other as humans (Mark 12:31).

5.   The Bible gives us at least five modes for relating to the rest of creation [as per above]:
   •   **Dominion** [Gen.1:26-28] "authority to tread creation underfoot," is *not* to be abused. However, we should not try to dilute the meaning of scripture here and thus diminish the level

of trust God has risked placing in us by giving such power over his creation, but rather use it as he wishes.

- **Priesthood** [Psa.150:6] *Let everything that has breath praise the LORD. Praise God.* The role of an OT priest offered things to God. The NT teaches the priesthood of all believers, i.e. we are to offer everything to God, enabling all creatures and habitats to function as God designed to his glory.

- **Companionship** [Prov.12:10] *having regard (sensitivity) towards creatures needs.* The word "companionship" carries the idea of "all eating bread together." We are not to perceive ourselves as outsiders observing and manipulating the rest of creation at will, but rather as humans we are also an integral part of creation, sharing friendship as should a farmer and draft animal, or a shepherd and sheepdog, and the sheep.

- **Stewardship** [Luke 16:2] We are accountable for what we do with God-given resources. We are placed as managers or overseers of all resources to use them and conserve them. Oikonomia (economy) means "careful administration of all creation for the long-term benefit of all."

- **Teamwork** [1 Cor.3:9] We have complementary roles under God to care properly. Together, we can achieve when each person discovers their own unique gifting by God and loyally pursues their calling with humility, seeking to consider how their role fits with those of others in a team (Phil.2:4). Leaders must encourage talents and delegate.

6. Each person's behaviour towards creation when aggregated together is responsible for the overall state of creation, including deforestation, global warming, pollution, poverty, and fear, so we must think communally and act correctly as individuals. The environmental impact of our lifestyle choices and behaviours is

a spiritual matter of eternal as well as of temporal significance. Christians who say "we are getting a new earth, so why divert our attention from preaching to care for this one" are sadly missing the fullness of the gospel and the Biblical mandate towards creation. The challenge for Christians is to work towards the restored relationships ("as at the beginning") envisioned by Isaiah 58:6-11 and 65:17-25. This entails perceiving ourselves as an integral part of creation as well as being souls in need of eternal salvation.

7. To separate salvation from creation diminishes the Biblical reality taught for both. They are integral and our mission towards creation can be summed up as *To let everything that has breath* – creatures and humans alike – *praise the LORD* i.e. to bring them to a point where they can express their God-given capacity to praisehim, which involves salvation. It is then that we shall be free to"praise the LORD too" (Psalm 150:6).

8. Wholistic development seeks to integrate the following aspects within a context of proper, Biblically-inspired Environmental Management for Ecosystem Security:

    a. Sustainable livelihoods - also allowing for future generations, and including health

    b. Natural resource management along conservation lines with balanced biodiversity

    c. Food security - based on adequate quantity, quality, local sovereignty, food cultures

    d. Land heritage – celebrating and maintaining the connection between people and land

    e. Specific resource monitoring and conservation – notably water and fuel sources

    f.   Geopolitical security to counteract tendencies towards an increasingly turbulent world

9.   Mobilising churches and communities to recognise environmental issues affecting them and enabling responses that address these effectively may include:

    a.   helping establish *FARMS* (Farm Asset Resource Management Study) and other livelihood groups (e.g. of potters, of weavers – like old craft guilds)

    b.   enabling churches in a *Christian Stewardship* review process, including environmental audit

    c.   encouraging understanding and use of under-utilised natural resources (e.g. plants as medicines)

    d.   addressing issues of displacement (refugees, migrants, labour, unemployment)

    e.   addressing issues of 'resource wars' with conflict resolution and peace-building approaches

    f.   demonstrating best environmental practices – soil, habitat, crop and animal husbandry

    g.   adoption of appropriate technologies such as fuel-saving stoves, tip-taps, pit latrines…

    h.   advocating environmental improvement schemes for community-building and morale-boosting.

God has provided two "books" by which he desires to reveal himself to us – the Bible and Creation. Thus, in our engagement with environmental matters, we are not only concerned to encourage improved management – to *occupy until the Lord comes* (Luke 19:13) – but also to demonstrate a thorough appreciation of creation, of nature. This means creation as "'speaking of God the Creator" and of his love for creation in its own right as well as through it toward us for communal delight and provision. Rediscovery of due wonder is heartening!

Signs of Environmental Responsibility

How should a well-managed place look? The appearance of land and property of churches, organisations, individuals, families and communities reflects the attitudes of members. A well-managed environment should have:

- Water supplies clean, roof water collected, protected from contamination and pollution
- Litter (polybags..) removed; organic waste composted, non-biodegradable waste disposed
- Trees and plantings are attractive and well-sited for shade and amenity
- Well-fenced, well-weeded ground with soil conserved, crops well-tended (Prov.24:24-30)
- Livestock controlled, well-fed and watered, contented and as healthy as possible
- Buildings, pathways and public spaces are maintained in a tidy, hygienic way
- Youths and other community groups mobilised to clean up litter and beautify their place
- "Best-kept village/township" competitions to help foster civic pride, communal caring
- An "environmental audit" to optimise local sourcing of food, minimise waste, encourage better natural resource management and sharing.

Ecosystem Security

Agriculture in its widest sense sits at the heart of man's relationship under God with nature and our natural environment. Farming is an integral part of sound environmental management. For everyone, that integrated ecosystem in which farming is central must provide a comprehensive **ecosystem security** which consists of: water security + food security + energy security + livelihood security + geopolitical security. In other words, ecosystem security must take account of all factors relevant to life on earth with agriculture having a crucial role. Thus food production is an essential ecosystem service to be included within that comprehensive portfolio.

The following points are offered regarding sub-Saharan Africa and elsewhere:

- Maintaining Ecosystem Security is the key objective of intergenerational farming
- Agro-ecological systems are the context to develop, conserve and pursue
- Improved integral management for higher outputs must retain farmer sovereignty
- Adoption of appropriate technologies - such as conservation farming - works
- *FARMS* (Farm Asset Resource Management Study) Groups suit farmer-learning
- Voluntary collaboration by farmers based on mutual trust works by shared learning
- Farmer networks assist independent, farmer-led extension information flow
- Farmer solidarity gains by farmer associations acting/advocating together worldwide

- We can learn from moves towards "re-peasantisation" as in Spain
- Farming families need "succession" plans - helped by objective, friendly outsiders.

If the above are concertedly embraced by policy-makers and farming communities alike, then there is hope that the rate of loss of the world's 500 million farming families can be attenuated and young entrants to farming encouraged. Thus, geopolitical stability prospects for sub-Saharan Africa and elsewhere would be enhanced, while failure to conserve family farms threatens global ecosystem security (Fig.8).

**Figure 8. Dynamics between Family & Farm
at the Heart of Global Ecosystem Security**

Geopolitical Context
Macro-Economic Context & Tenure

| ETHICS | EQUITY | ENERGY-EFFICIENCY |

FAMILY ⟷ FARM

| ECOLOGY | ECONOMICS | EMPLOYMENT |

Global Harmony Aspirations

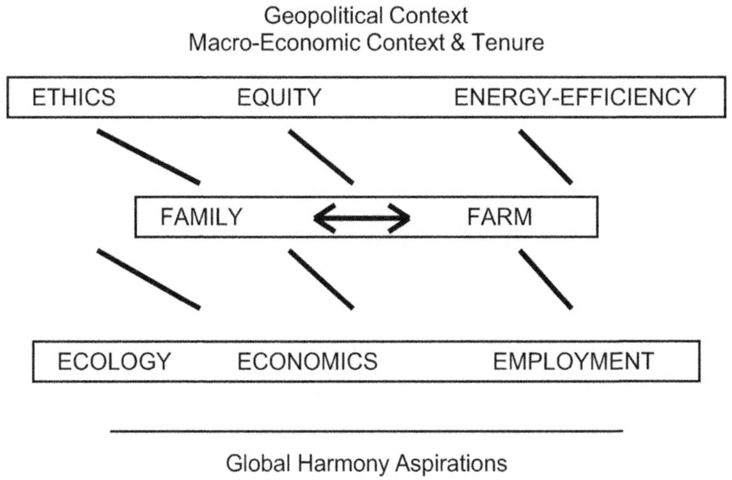

Climate Change

Current global warming trends, with more GHGs (Greenhouse Gases) and rising sea levels are giving consequent increases in the severity and unpredictability of the weather. Consensus is considerable that substantial contribution is made to it by human activity. Agriculture, including livestock production in particular, contributes its share to global warming. Agricultural implications may include suffering or gain from climate change depending geographically upon where one is farming. In general, already marginal food insecure areas will suffer most – notably in sub-Saharan Africa. Moral dilemmas are raised not only by the events resulting and likely to result from climate change but also from the actual and potential responses to it at both policy and personal levels. Practical responses – not panic - need to be considered and applied at home and internationally. We must remember that God has given us an inherently stable earth, promising that while it remains, seedtime & harvest, cold & heat, summer & winter, day & night will not cease (Gen.8:22).

Greater poverty impacts agriculture hugely since it hampers human energy/effort to plant and restricts capacity to afford necessary inputs. Over 40% of the world's people are unable or barely able to meet their survival needs. Climate change threatens to make the Sustainable Development Goals unattainable. It will result in greater poverty, wider discrepancy between rich and poor, sea level rises, and more precarious livelihoods challenging survival. Already, some 2.7 billion people try to live on £1 or less per day. Action on climate change is integral to poverty reduction. Such action requires both **mitigation** of the rate of change and **adaptation** to change that does occur. Stabilising CO^2 at 450 ppm (requiring cuts of 60-90% in GHG emissions before 2100) may limit the mean global temperature rise to <2°C. Mitigation of climate change is affordable; to stabilise at 450 ppm CO^2 would cost 1-4% of global average GDP over 50 years. Justice and equity demand action is taken.

Climate change has important implications for food production, processing and distribution and thus for food security. Agriculture contributes towards climate change as well as both suffering from it and potentially in some areas benefiting from it. Farming people are calculating their carbon footprints, in order not only to mitigate them but also to make business sense of their impacts. According to Stern (2006) global "greenhouse gas" (GHG) emissions arose from the major sources listed as follows:- Power stations 24%; Land misuse – mainly deforestation 18% (Brazil led on this = 3.1Mha between 2000-2005, followed by Indonesia = 1.8 Mha); Transport, including aviation 14%; Agriculture 14%; Industry 14%; Fuel used in buildings 8%.

Livestock production contributes almost 80% of agriculture's total GHG emissions. This arises from deforestation to create pastures, emissions from livestock manures especially of nitrous oxide, and methane originating from rumen fermentation (25% of it from dairy cows). However, mitigation consists in keeping livestock in integrated mixed farming systems. Cattle raised in huge feedlots where rainforest once thrived become the worst culprits. As people become wealthier, they tend to consume more dairy products and meat, especially red meat (from ruminants). Policy attention to this is recommended on health grounds, notably its tendency to increase ischaemic heart disease, obesity and colo-rectal cancer. Current global daily consumption of all meats averages some 100g per person though this varies by ten-fold between the lowest and highest consumption figures (e.g. Africa 31g; "developed" countries 224g). A daily target of 90g per person maximum is considered reasonable by dieticians, with not more than 50g as red meat. Apart from health gains, eating more chicken and vegetarian-farmed fish would reduce agriculture's output of methane and protect wild fish stocks. Eating more crop products is more efficient in delivering overall dietary supplies, bearing in mind that currently around one person in eight still goes to bed hungry each night. Poor and food-insecure countries could lose 10-20% of their cereal production owing to climate change.

Oil is getting scarce; airfreight uses some 60 times the energy of sea transport and trucks use some 10 times the energy of trains per tonne carried, while boxed, processed cereals such as *Corn Flakes* contain less than one-sixth of the energy it takes to produce them. By contrast, most of the energy the maize contains is conserved if eaten locally as by the typical tropical grower of maize who roasts her own cobs locally, especially if – relatively unusually – she uses a fuel-saving stove. Feeding the average American takes around 1800 litres of oil equivalent per year. Principal usage of energy within North American agronomy is reckoned as: 33% fertilisers; 20% machinery operation; 16% transport; 13% irrigation; 5% biocides. Each tonne of the world's commonest straight nitrogen fertiliser (AN, ammonium nitrate) requires some five tonnes of oil to produce. Some 10% of US national energy use is within agriculture. A global move to sustainable agriculture for sustainable development is clearly vital. International policy targets are for GHG emissions from agriculture by 2050 to be no more than those for 2005, and overall to achieve net zero carbon to the atmosphere.

Practical responses are particularly urgent for Africa where climate change threatens the livelihoods (including food security) of many poor people. Helping poor people to adapt (through research on adaptive crop cultivars, appropriate technologies, strategies and institutions) is imperative. Rainfed agricultural output in some African countries is dropping significantly. For instance, Niger - over five times the size of the UK - already has >80% of its total area as desert and under 3% is cultivable. Millet yields have declined to some 90% of those attained 50 years ago while average sorghum yields are now only 20% of those achieved half a century ago. The 600mm per annum isohyet (line on a map joining places of that rainfall level) is receding towards the southern border with Nigeria, further limiting cultivable land. Hope placed in irrigation for rice and vegetables has to be tempered by concerns for careful management regarding the potential speed of salinisation. Countries at comparable latitudes south of the equator in Africa are likely to suffer similarly increased constraints. Niger's current population (in 2021) of 25 million is projected to rise to between 43 and 77 million by 2050, depending on the success or otherwise of birth control measures adopted. According to culture, many of the extra people will wish to keep more cattle, goats and sheep. However, albeit under much more favourable rainfall conditions, *Send-A-Cow* in Uganda (www.sendacow.org.uk) has done studies showing huge positive impacts of a single cow or dairy goat on Farm-Household System vitality and viability – and in such integrated systems that the carbon-footprint (notably methane + manure) is offset by recycling, by fodder crops and by tree planting so that over 5 years it is 2.5 times positive in carbon capture! Alongside fuel-efficient moulded mud stoves, more tree planting is also needed.

Water Security

Several key questions are important regarding water as a resource:

- What research on local ecology, especially hydrology, has been done?
- Is rainwater storage possible?
- Are surface water improvements available?
- Are communities educated in basic hygiene?
- Are socio-economic and technical aspects being properly linked?
- Are local groups being trained in construction, maintenance and repair?
- Has slow sand filtration been considered?
- How can groundwater be extracted?

- What sources are available? Water sources may include:- rainwater via roofs; protected springs; wells – hand-dug, driven or bored tubes, jetted tubes; boreholes, dams, tanks

Water quantities and quality requirements are approximately as follows:

- Human use: c.25 litres/person/day globally
- Farmland use: c.100,000 litres/hectare irrigated globally
- Physical quality – minimal suspended solids
- Chemical quality – Na+ <200 ppm; Cl- <500 ppm; NO^3- <10 ppm
- Biological quality – nil faecal coliforms, nil schistosome, eggs, etc..

Biochemical Oxygen Demand (BOD) should be < 1mg/litre in a clean river but goes up to 600 mg/litre in raw sewage... treated sewage gets to < 20 mg/litre; discharge standards apply in countries with due governance of these matters.

Droughts, floods and increasingly erratic rains characterise the global climate of the 21st century. The term "resource wars" entered the international management vocabulary around 1980 in regard to the capture and control of water catchments. This is seen as motivating many land grabs. Some 9 out of 10 of the world's people have access to "improved" water supplies, with huge variations: from 93% in India - meaning that 90 million people there do *not* have such access, to 33% in Somalia where 6.5 million people do *not* have access to improved water sources. Arguably, water security is the priority within ecosystem security along with food, energy, livelihoods and geopolitical security. It is the most crucial element within natural capital and requires judicious management for both quantity and quality. Improved water management is likely to gain rewards within environmental land management and water catchment policies worldwide.

Agriculture uses over 70% of the world's water, notably for irrigation. This must be efficient. On a smaller scale, careful irrigation may include collecting roof-water, building local small-scale dams – notably sand-dams, using bucket-lines with drip irrigation for vegetables, and micro-catchment rainwater harvesting. On a larger field-scale, drip irrigation as developed in Israel during the 1960s and 1970s offers a means of effective water rationing, along with some of the pioneering precision agriculture now much vaunted by agritech proposals. Impressive field-level doubling or more of yields is being achieved on a huge scale through conservation farming, the effectiveness of which is substantially based on water conservation within the soil, coupled with disciplined crop management (Kassam, 2020). Livestock farming uses water too: processing a chicken to market consumes some 28 litres of water in Brazil!

Integral water management

• This can supply domestic and agricultural water requirements while simultaneously yielding fish from reservoirs, energy via hydro-electricity and supporting sustainable tourism including sport fishing. Some 72% of the earth's surface is ocean and some two-thirds of this has been historically classified as "high seas" where no nation is designated to manage it. All nations need to support the UN Global Ocean Commission and the IMO (International Marine Organisation), and initiatives such as 2015-25 Decade of African Seas and Oceans, which seeks to regenerate oceans for the benefit of all, including regulating illegal and exploitative industrial fishing.

Fish Farming

• Oceans are being over-fished. The present writer's interest in fish farming began in the mid-1970s when we lived close to the Panyam

Fish Farm, Nigeria, then said to be Africa's largest at 309 ha. Under Government control since its establishment in the 1950s by Austrians using *Cyprinus carpio,* it became so moribund by 2016 that the Plateau State Government entered a Public-Private Partnership with Solbec Ltd in an attempt to resuscitate the internally generated revenue (IGR) of Plateau State Government. It is reckoned to have the capacity to produce about 4.9 tonnes of fish per hectare and over 10 million fingerlings annually. Plateau State also has about 20 dams and reservoirs with an estimated water surface area of 673 hectares, as well as 12 natural lakes with a water surface area of about 365 hectares. In addition, of over 1,000 abandoned mining ponds in the State, already 24 have been certified fit for fish production. Fish farming observed and encouraged elsewhere, in both East and Southern Africa and India, has featured notably *Tilapia.* Tilapia can be grown in combination with deep-water paddy rice, or with retted cassava (soaked to remove its toxins) when Tilapia can yield 4t/ ha/yr. A rice paddy can also be a good nursery for growing fry to 30g. Animal pens can be built over ponds to supply manures - pigs and poultry being both commonly used so that Tilapia suit integrated farming systems of various sorts, as done long ago in traditional Chinese farming systems! Let's integrate water and fish better now! Let's also care internationally for mangroves which provide nurseries for many ocean fish.

Water & Sanitation - the key questions

- Does it involve/educate local people? Washing hands + soap can cut deaths by 33%
- Is latrine type linked to local geology, avoiding contamination of nearby water points?
- Are VIP (Ventilated Improved Pit) latrines affordable?

- Is planning for shallower pit latrine filling before planting with bananas appropriate?
- Is there a safe linkage to nutrient capture in composting?
- Have all possibilities been considered re: deposition, collection, transport, treatment?

Diarrhoea is the most important public health problem directly related to water and sanitation. About 4 million cases of diarrhoea per year cause 1.8 million deaths, over 90 per cent of them (1.6 million) among children under five. Repeated episodes of diarrhoeal disease make children more vulnerable to other diseases and malnutrition. The simple act of washing hands with soap and water can cut diarrhoeal disease by one-third. Next to providing adequate sanitation facilities, it is the key to preventing waterborne diseases:

- Cholera is an acute diarrhoeal disease that can kill within hours if left untreated.
- Up to 80% of cases can be successfully treated with oral rehydration salts + sugar.
- Effective control measures rely on prevention, preparedness and response.
- Provision of safe water and sanitation is critical in reducing the impact of cholera and other waterborne diseases.
- Oral cholera vaccines are considered an additional means to control cholera, but should not replace conventional control measures.

Worldwide, some 800 million individuals lack access to improved drinking-water, and one person in three lacks improved sanitation.

Energy Security
Energy is required for power generation to drive machinery in manufacturing and transport, to heat and to cool homes, to produce

and to cook food. Energy is ultimately derived from the sun via photosynthesis, from flowing water in rivers and tides via mill-wheels and turbines – including those driven by wind, although wind is erratic. Historically, draft animal power has often provided first steps in village mechanisation. Arguably, draft animals offer the most appropriate level of development in this regard since they are renewable, provide manure rather than consuming fossil fuels and are edible provided they are slaughtered before too old and tough - they are often eaten too old, necessitating a pressure cooker and good sauce! Horace (Rome, 65-8 BC) averred:

> Happy the man who, far from schemes of business, like the early generations of mankind, ploughs and ploughs again his ancestral furrow, with oxen of his own breeding, and no yoke of usury [extortionate interest payments] about his neck.

Draft animals retain huge economic and strategic value in international agriculture, especially in the tropics. In many dryland cultures, the acquisition of a donkey to carry water is a pre-requisite before inviting a wife and building a home! Much of India's paddy rice land is still cultivated using oxen. Draft animals are used to work between tree crops in the tropics, such as ox-drawn weeders between coffee and banana rows in Kenya. Other draft animals are locally common, including camels in North Africa and elephants in SW India. Working dogs feature elsewhere in pulling power. The relationship between draft animal and farmer is vital requiring mutual understanding, appropriate training and extension concerning both. They remain of strategic importance widely, not least as oxen for hire to plough land for small-scale farmers in East Africa.

Nuclear power is increasingly important globally and is clean with the crucial exception that its waste is highly and persistently toxic. As in all matters, the fear of the LORD is the beginning of wisdom.

The second law of thermodynamics describes the tendency of energy to dissipate, while agriculture aims to concentrate useful energy within crops and farming systems. A key question is how efficiently this can be done while simultaneously respecting God's creation and caring as He cares. What then is agricultural efficiency?:

- Output (tonnes/ha)? ; Value (£/ha)?; Output (t or £) per person employed)?
- If the last, then improvement is by increasing yield and/or decreasing labour...
- The bicycle is one of the most efficient machines; its efficiency is based on the ratio between energy applied to the pedals, and energy delivered through the wheels to move forward...
- Agricultural efficiency is most usefully defined as the ratio between total energy invested per hectare starting with soil preparation compared with the total energy available from that hectare as food on the plate = SOIL to PLATE!
- Thus it takes account of the total energy cost of field operations and of producing and delivering all inputs, of processing, packaging and transporting all outputs.
- Efficiency defined in these real terms increases with the localisation of the farming system.

Energy efficiency needs to become the accepted baseline technical criterion for comparing alternative agricultural systems for productivity (measured in terms of the ratio of output per unit of input) and in encouraging and evaluating integrated rural development and resilience. Energy efficiency on a planetary scale needs analysis and monitoring, with best practice guidelines. Renewable energy sources, notably micro-hydro and solar panels on farm buildings and farm houses, need an enabling planning environment and encouragement from governments and NGOs. One small solar panel on a small, remote homestead roof can transform life for its occupants, enabling charging of mobile telephone batteries, providing light and enabling the use of a laptop computer for learning and communication. Farm-Household Systems of small, integrated, mixed farms supplying local food are among the most energy-efficient farms in the world, and are to be conserved and encouraged.

It is necessary to beware of biofuel crops, intrusively sited wind turbines, and solar-panelled arable fields when reasonably priced food is increasingly important worldwide. Renewable energy that conflicts with priority land uses needs to be catalogued, researched, and given strategic appraisal and management. Although some under grazing by sheep and goats is possible, covering productive fields with solar panels exacerbates the loss of farmland, notwithstanding their sound short-term business sense given various governments' energy grants, and appeal of generating renewable energy towards net zero carbon targets. Soil carbon sequestration and emissions should be accounted for separately. The one should never be netted out against the other. 100% of carbon taxes collected, at both the farm level and the input manufacture level, could be refunded to farmers.

Although it has become fashionable to criticise cattle and to claim they are energy-inefficient, this is incorrect. Not only does the LORD own the cattle on a thousand hills (Psa.50:10) but he loves cattle, as he reminded Jonah (4:11). There is a strong case *for* cattle. Cattle are essential components of healthy grassland ecosystems that build soil and capture carbon; they enable us to produce food on land that could otherwise not produce food or that should not be cropped; and they are part of sustainable, nutrient-cycling mixed farming operations, as well as draft-power providers in some cases. Atmospheric methane levels can be stabilised and even reduced while cattle production continues (though restructuring will be needed to remove corporate-controlled, output-maximising cattle production systems such as feedlots using hormones in feeds too). In this way, the net incomes of cattle producers and the number of family farmers raising cattle can be maintained sensibly.

Food Security

Integral Mission is about expressing and implementing the rich wholeness of the Christian good news by thoughts, words and actions. The Lord's Prayer instructs requesting physical bread in the context of spiritual requests (Matt.6:11). The Bible teaches God's intended integration of physical and spiritual bread – *man does not live on bread alone but on every word that comes from the mouth of the LORD.* (Deut. 8:3; Matt.4:4; Luke 4:4). Companionship is promoted by taking bread together.

Food security is not an absolute concept eliminating trade but rather a relative concept increasing the following:

a. Availability of adequate quantity and quality of locally-grown agricultural produce,
b. Accessibility of supplies for urban/land-remote areas (food attainable and affordable),
c. Appreciation of the close link between nutrition and health for work and enjoyment,
d. Avoidance of undue risk from livelihood vulnerability, oil-dependence, hazard and shock.

Food security depends upon respect for the land and natural resources as God-given, covenanted assets rather than as contextless space for technological exploitation. Creation is designed for harmonious relationships between God, humans and other creatures. Oikonomia (economy) is properly defined as "managing all creation for the benefit of all creation." "Food Sovereignty" means local control and determination of policy over food production and supplies, and is not to be confused with food security. Within this context, food security needs to be considered at household, village, national and international levels.

Factors affecting Food Security

• Spiritual – Biblical foundations need to be revisited, affirmed and pursued in practice
   The Earth is the LORD's, and everything in it. - Psalm 24:1; relieve hunger.
• Supply - Majority of food supply needs to grow as close to consumers as possible
   True food security is not simply the ability to buy but to grow and store locally.
• Significance - Proportion of income spent on food needs to reflect real cost/value
   It is misleading to measure poorer countries as spending >75% and poorest 100% on food.
• Sourcing - Local sourcing needs to be maximised to link with protection and security
   Food miles, air pollution, global warming and oil-dependence have all become excessive.
• Safety - Food must be safe to consume in quality, dietary diversity, and seasonality
   We need to conserve and celebrate our food cultures; shun junk food and avoid obesity.
• Sustainability - Systems must be long-term viable to provide for future generations

Sustainable livelihoods mean environmental care and local diet sourcing.

- System - Whole food/farming systems need to be well managed and integrated

Integrated realism is needed in rural management; working farmers possess this quality.

A sustainable food security policy needs to enable farmers to farm and to be internationally encouraged in it. However, within that, nation states must be enabled to have more control over their own food supply policies (to exercise food sovereignty). An International *"Highway Code"* for trading is needed to regulate excessive movement especially of staple foods such as rice, maize and chickens into areas where they can perfectly well be grown for viable livelihoods locally if not swamped by cheap imports. Food security is central to livelihood viability since without adequate nutrition working ability is impaired, without work HIV/AIDS still spreads, and without reliable local food supplies, peace and stability in society are threatened. Thus Ecosystem Security integrates sustainable management for Food + Water + Energy + Livelihoods + Geopolitical Stability.

Practical Food Security

On which training workshops and courses are offered. This involves sound management, carried out as locally as possible, at all stages of:

1. **Field and farm production** using sustainable farming systems with sound nutrient management, integrated mixed cropping and livestock.
2. **Crop and livestock produce storage** in clean, safe stores at both household, village, regional, national and international levels.

3. **Processing** using the asset of solar drying as well as other preservation techniques (including pickling, bottling and jam-making) for fruits, vegetables and other surplus produce, which is often wasted while the household later in the year suffers shortage.

4. **Marketing** of produce, with as much value added locally by the producer as possible.

5. **Farmer collaboration** encouraged through the formation of *FARMS* Groups (**Farm Asset Resource Management Study** Groups) to learn from one another.

FOOD SECURITY & INTEGRAL MISSION

Faith and food are intertwined in God's Economy;
To pray's to work, to work's to pray – integral harmony.
The Lord Himself instructed prayer for daily bread to say;
"Companionship" – "together bread" communion display.

The link of faith and food supply in Genesis is told
Through Joseph's wisdom heaven
sent, and blessings shared untold,
And manna in the desert God's provision from on high
Confirmed mankind's dependence on eternity's supply.

'Tis very elemental photosynthesis to catch
When simply sowing seeds within a vegetable patch;
When milking cows, collecting eggs and fishing are well done
'Tis clear co-operation shown by which our food is won.

To each it matters daily to be physically fed
And yet Eight-Fifty million still go hungry to their bed,
So true integral mission now cannot ignore our food
Amount, and where and how it's grown, must quality include.

Environmental damage we by wrong food systems cause,
Unnecessary trading damage gathers no applause,
For those producing strive for more to keep their prices low
And at the destination imports cause small farms to go.

There is Divine connection between us and land and food,
The vision of Micah 4:4 should not now be eschewed,
And yet with growing refugees and migrants more each day
'Under one's tree without a fear' seems further yet away.

The "Bread of Life" is Jesus who did also share our bread
In mission's integral display, not either/or instead:
Will we take food security as mission charge today
And manage God's creation with evangelism, pray?

Land Matters

The Psalmist (Psa.115:16) declares, *The highest heavens belong to the LORD, but the earth has He given to the human race.* As Acts 17:26 records,

> *From one man he made all the nations, that they should inhabit the whole earth; and he marked out their appointed times in history and the boundaries of their lands.*

Whatever the local system of land tenure and the historic records of a culture, those two facts of creation remain: we are tenants of earth, not its owners; we all have the same life-blood.

In this context, we note that there is so much conflict over land in the world to this day. Within it, and very much affecting Africa, is the growing incidence of "land-grabbing." Land consists of a living soil ecosystem underpinning nature and needs to be valued as such. Land management is the basis for life. Soil fertility sustains human livelihoods against poverty. Land tenure is the heritage of particular communities or nations; "land grab" threatens it.

Land resources merit particular evaluation at this time in sub-Saharan Africa (SSA) and elsewhere in the tropics when soil fertility is increasingly vital for food security and climate change mitigation. The financial crisis affecting many countries has made them desperate to generate funds by any means possible, including the irrevocable sale or long-term lease of land. Simultaneously, previous speculators on failing financial markets now gamble on food and land. The ensuing so-called "land grab" is a burgeoning phenomenon with huge socio-economic livelihood and geopolitical consequences.

Communal land tenure has characterised most of Africa, with custom rather than legal contract determining tenure and its continuance. 'Roman' law is increasingly dominant whereby land can be bought, sold and leased with contractual documents overriding indigenous custom and stewardship. This has opened the floodgates to abuse and unfavourable land-grabbing as well as to some genuinely beneficial investment, such as for rainforest protection. Overall, it is an agricultural justice issue, requiring land equity.

Though some land is underutilised, globally very little land is vacant, unused or not owned in some way. Land deals need to be made with better and transparent guidelines. Though many agreements contain promises of financial investments to benefit the host country, local jobs, technology transfer and income generation opportunities there is little evidence of their fulfilment. Land grabs of large tracts that displace smallholder farmers, pastoralists and whole communities of indigenous people should be vigorously opposed and brought to light. However, some investments in agriculture by outsiders can benefit local communities and have been set up collaboratively by due legal process. Africa's economy is ripe for general upliftment but must not be hijacked. Foreign investors are of different kinds. There are at least three types:

a.   blatantly exploitative profiteers;
b.   innovative entrepreneurs;
c.   socially and/or environmentally responsible philanthropically inclined stewards.

It is possible to aim for mutually beneficial and sustainable business partnerships between responsible investors in African agriculture, local people and their governments - which often lack enough capital. Promoting these involves not only mobilising world opinion against 'land grabbing' and towards them, but also reinforcing AU/ UN guidelines (Fig.9). These guidelines offer a framework for useful discussion internationally but are not enforceable, can only be voluntary and thus many think them grossly inadequate and open to abuse by governments and trans-national corporations.

**Figure 9. Guidelines for more Equitable
Land Investment (after Liversage, 2011).**

i.	existing rights to land and natural resources must be recognised and respected;
ii.	investments must not jeopardise food security but rather strengthen it;
iii.	processes for accessing land and making associated investments must be transparent, monitored, and ensure accountability by all stakeholders, thereby improving the business, legal & regulatory environment;
iv.	all those materially affected must be consulted and agreements from consultations recorded and enforced;
v.	projects must be economically viable, respect the rule of law, reflect industry best practice and result in durable shared value;
vi.	investments must generate desirable social and distributional impacts, and must not increase vulnerability;
vii.	environmental impacts must be quantified and measures taken to encourage sustainable resource use while minimising and mitigating negative impacts.

Liversage (2011) suggests more responsible approaches towards investment in agriculture by outsiders, which respect the main investors - the world's 500 million or so smallholder farm families:

> ...enabling poor rural people to be part of the solution for global food security must be a priority for governments, the international development community and any other investors.

Women's empowerment is crucial. Women achieve a majority of tropical agricultural production. In Malawi, for instance, mostly female smallholders cultivate between 0.5-1.0 hectares, with some 70% of cultivated land devoted to maize. Such mono-cropping depletes soil fertility. On harvested maize, women spend countless further hours preparing *nsima* very fine flour after removing the more nutritious coarse matter. Access to land is key for food security and sustainable livelihoods in Malawi. Around 70% of Malawians are reckoned below the poverty line with 90% of them in rural areas. The hunger season is from December to February, with many missing a whole day's meals, and most consuming under two meals per day. This calls not only for more production and better nutrition but also for practical food preservation, storage and processing to reduce food wastage.

Overall, in Africa and elsewhere, the "food security army" of smallholder farmers need greater advocacy, help in improving their own soil management and livelihood sustainability, and fairer trading as well as better protection from predatory land acquisitions both from within and outside their home country's borders.

Sustainable Agriculture

Agriculture is central to sustainable economies throughout the world, and notably in sub-Saharan Africa both to produce food and other raw materials, and to manage tidy landscapes.

Agriculture provides the principal livelihood for most Africans, and for one in three people globally. It has sustained rural survival to date, though sometimes within challenging and unpredictably harsh environments.

Farmers perform crucial roles for society as producers, as stewards of natural resources, as rural skill-holders, as landscape custodians, as hosts for visitors to rural areas, as community members and as employers. "Farmer conservation" is a legitimate policy aspiration and objective for Africa and beyond, enabling the retention of enough farmers in place to deliver these benefits.

Features of sustainable agriculture include certain guidelines and field practices:

• Good soil conservation that also achieves [and is promoted as] good water catchment;

- Feeding the soil: recycling nutrients, maintaining growth-conducive soil conditions;
- Mixing & /or rotating crops of different plant families to limit weeds, pests & diseases;
- Reduced & timely cultivations with correct spacing & depth of planting for each crop;
- Integrating livestock to use crop by-products, to produce manures/ enrich composts;
- Use of human urine is an opportunity; faeces can also be composted with great care;
- Encouraging sharing of experience and wisdom of local farmers for mutual progress.

Attainment of sustainability is vital internationally in order to maintain and deliver:

a. Conserved biodiverse (species-rich) landscapes - [already done by the best farmers]
b. "Commonwealth" integrated economies - maximising local interdependence
c. Networks of relational communities i.e. where good relationships are strengthened.

Sustainability is a comprehensive concept with at least 12 criteria suggested here - the 12 Es. Sustainability must simultaneously satisfy six essential (**E**) criteria:

a. *Economy* - managing all creation's resources for the benefit of all creation
b. *Ecology* - balanced care of the environment and its associated flora, fauna and people.

c.   *Equity* - pursuit of justice for all in a shared earth of shared wealth NOT shared poverty

d.   *Energy-Efficiency* - wasting much less energy in farming & food delivery systems

e.   *Employment* - promoting creative employment to secure local farm product supply

f.   *Ethics* - guidance to do what is good, fair and right in relation to God's perspectives.

All these require six *promoter* (e) criteria: **education, enterprise, enthusiasm, effort-effectiveness, expectancy** of some reward/ success, leading to **enjoyment** of living on a worldwide basis. All may be put together in the context of the Cross (Fig.10):

**Figure 10. Essentials and Promoters
of Development in the Cross**

e **E** e

E E E

e **E** e

e **E** e

These 12 Es can be used as a kind of template or checklist against which a particular agricultural system may be evaluated. In general, if this is done, it is impossible to escape the conclusion that the thrust driving agriculture worldwide has to change. Present policy, especially that of the WTO on trading is patently not sustainable for farmed or wild species, for farmers or for people (consumers – all of us) in general. However, many agricultural systems delivering sustainability already exist in practice. Good farmers merit greater respect.

Agrarian advocacy is needed simultaneously to integrate sustainable farm livelihoods, natural resource management, food security and land heritage connections everywhere. Farmer conservation coupled with the encouragement of farmer collaboration are crucial since only practical farmers possess the integrated realism to implement these interdependent pursuits. Sustainable agriculture requires collective humility and repentance, followed by disciplined farming bringing *healing to the land* (2 Chron.7:14).

Farms Groups

These are **F**arm **A**sset **R**esource **M**anagement Study Groups. The author has been encouraging the formation of *FARMS* **Groups** at the community level, including with those Christians who are farmers inviting their neighbours to learn together and to share their farming challenges, problems and solutions. Other livelihood groups may meet too e.g. weavers. As we learn together, farming can progress, trust can develop, and our neighbours may find the love of God in Christ for them within everyday life.

Why the name "FARMS" Groups? Because all farmers have faced the challenge of business survival in recent years and need to assess ALL their farms' assets as potential resources for improved management in order to gain a sustainable livelihood. All over the world, farmers prefer to learn from other farmers (practitioners of any kind prefer to learn from other practitioners – nurses from nurses, and so on). Therefore, study together in practically-focused groups with farmer-chosen agenda provides a suitable opportunity for this and for trust to grow without which any sort of collaborative business cooperation cannot work. Such future collaboration may be in the interests of group members BUT they must decide if this is to be so after they have come to know and trust each other - which happens most naturally during learning together.

What makes such a group work? It needs to be:

a.   outsider "sparked" only; NEVER imposed NOR coerced into existence.

b.   farmer owned and locally led, ideally with spouses welcome too.

c.   self-running (autonomous) - with someone to co-ordinate meetings.

d.   small enough to be intimate but large enough to give a creative mix (say 12-25).

e.   ideally holding on-farm and field meetings, or at least practical discussions.

f.   including taking a simple meal together during the meeting.

g.   promoting the fun element of meeting together.

h.   promoting "belonging" but welcoming newcomers.

i.   encouraging overlarge groups to split and start a new one.

j.   fostering an outward-looking group culture.

k.   encouraging problem-sharing.

l.   stimulating solution-seeking.

m.   becoming more resource and market conscious and astute.

n.   developing its own identity/name.

o.   given time to gel (if it is going to do) - typically after around 20 meetings.

p.   ideally, area per group covering a maximum travel time of some 20-30 minutes.

q.   meeting ideally around ten times per year, avoiding busiest months but could be more often in a close village context.

Developing FARMS (Farm Asset ResourceManagement Study) Groups

Through *FARMS* Groups, apart from enjoyment and encouragement, hopefully members might further together "learn to earn." It takes some 20 meetings for any group to "gel" - to gain its own identity and a life of its own. Of course, some groups may never reach this stage. Successful groups need not last for ever. Coordination of such groups involves a catalyst/lubricant extension by the coordinator. The fact is that without the coordinator's initial catalysis, a *FARM's* groups may not start at all. Once it has begun, the role of the coordinator needs to be analogous to that of the lubricant in a well-running engine - noticed only when absent! This is Catalyst/Lubricant Extension. Any healthy group should regularly (perhaps annually) review :-

a.   whether it should continue to exist; it is better to stop while a thing is still going well!

b.   whether it welcomes new members with the fresh insights they may bring

c.   whether it has become too large and, if so, to consider "budding" a new group like a yeast.

d.   whether there are new potential ways of benefiting from collective group action such as making systematic enterprise or field comparisons (recording all field operations, physical and financial results); forming farmer-controlled businesses (FCBs) to combat big business power and be "local;" involvement in Farmers' Markets to strengthen communities, cut out middlemen, save energy; adding value to ex-farm raw products, with local branding and collaborative direct sales from farms to consumers; and many others.

Sustainable Forestry

Global forest area is some 90% natural and 10% planted. Forests cover some 30% of the world's land area, and Gabon in Africa leads the world in having the highest proportion of its territory under forest. Within Africa, Zambia has the greatest proportion of its land area under national environmental protection (over 40%). In Africa, the largest concentration of forest is found in the Congo basin covering some 1.3 million km². On the other hand, the fastest rates of deforestation recorded globally have been in Africa – in countries including Burundi and Nigeria. Malawi has become largely deforested with farmland and 'mango-savanna' instead, owing especially to huge wood fuel demands of the rising population, plus freely roaming goats in many areas. Informal surveys by the author of some 350 families in rural Malawi in 2006 indicated that the average family spent 30-35% of disposable monthly income on acquiring wood fuel, most of it burnt wastefully to cook on 3 large stones. This reinforces the importance of teaching about fuel-saving stoves and how to make them. A simple, portable stove can pay for its capital cost in wood saved within less than one month! Better still are those constructed from termite soil within kitchens and incorporating proper chimneys.

It can be reckoned using FAO data that:

- Forests are home to 300 million people around the world, formally employing 14M.
- More than 1.6 billion people depend to varying degrees on forests for their livelihoods, e.g. fuelwood, medicinal plants and forest foods.
- About 60 million indigenous people are almost wholly dependent on forests.
- Some 350 million people who live within or adjacent to dense forests depend on them to a high degree for subsistence and income.
- In developing countries, about 1.2 billion people rely on agroforestry farming systems that help to sustain agricultural productivity and generate income.
- Mangrove forests, which cover about 15 million hectares worldwide, are essential to the life cycles of the majority of the world's commercial fish species.

Trees should be valued at various levels - intrinsically as God's creation, as notable specimens and as landscape features, for their products, for their protection and for their global ecosystem role (Fig.11)

Figure 11. Levels of Value to Treasure in Trees

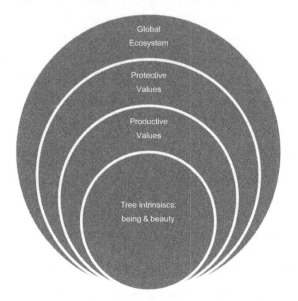

Development of sustainable forest industries is urgent, along with climate change mitigation and adaptation, and better recognition of value and protection for local forests.

The "Great Green Wall" of trees proposed in 2012 by Dennis Garrity of World Agroforestry Centre (formerly ICRAF; https:// www.worldagroforestry.org/" - *"Transforming Lives & Landscapes"*) will extend from the Senegalese coast to the Djibouti coast upon completion. It can be achieved when practices such as Evergreen Agriculture are used against desertification because its affordable, sustainable and accessible farming methods benefit not only rural smallholder farmers but also the environment, encouraging agro-ecological farming systems among the world's around 500 million farm families. To treasure trees, one needs to appreciate something of the rich international diversity of species. For instance, the evergreen red mahogany or *mbawa (Khaya anthotheca = K.nyassica)* is fittingly the national tree of Malawi. Also among Malawi's special trees is *Aleurites montana* (of *Euphorbiaceae)* introduced in 1931 as a source of tung oil exported for paints and varnishes. A splendid allegory of the value of tree planting has been published, republished and dramatised since it first appeared (Giono, 1954). The spiritual significance of trees perhaps relates in part to the fact that many of them and their associated forests far transcend the span of a human life. There are baobabs in Africa and olive trees in the Garden of Gethsemane in Jerusalem reckoned to exceed 3,000 years of age.

There are considerable Biblical references to trees, including several named species, and lessons drawn from them, from which we can derive both spiritual and physical lessons to apply to our lives, land and livelihoods. Taking the forbidden fruit of the Tree of Life in the Garden of Eden led to the fall of man (Gen.2:17; 3:1-9). In the book of Revelation, of all creatures, trees are singled out for protection alongside land and sea (Rev.7:3). In the final chapter of the Bible is the vision of the tree of life bearing twelve fruits in season and having leaves for the 'healing of the nations' (Rev.22:2, 14). Substantial healing now is possible using knowledge of the healing properties of various trees (see https://anamed.org/en/"). Reasons for growing and nurturing trees are manifold. They can both help halt desertification and also reclaim degraded land. Key productive and protective values of trees are depicted in Fig.12.

Figure 12. The Value of Trees[1]

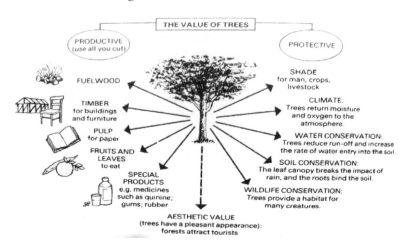

Humans are an integral part of forest and rural communities. However, indigenous and local communities, such as thousands in Ethiopia, are being forcibly relocated to make land available for investment in agriculture. There are plans to relocate very many more people, most of whom are subsistence farmers who have been able, until now, to feed their families without receiving government or foreign aid.

Created in 1959, the African Forestry Wildlife Commission (AFWC) is one of six Regional Forestry Commissions established by FAO to provide a policy and technical forum for countries to discuss and address forest issues on a regional basis. It meets every two years. The Nyika-Vwaza Trust affords habitat and wildlife protection not only within Malawi but across the border into Zambia. National organisations play a vital role, such as the Wildlife & Environmental Society of Malawi (WESM), as do civil society organisations that have become transnational such as the Green Belt Movement begun in 1977

---

[1](From Joy & Wibberley, 1979) NB Carbon sequestration omitted.

in Kenya by the late Wangari Maathai (2009) – though she began with her own small tree nursery in 1974. She saw engaging local farmers and their management skills, together with mobilisation by church leaders as key.

The principles for extension of tree planting adopted and field-tested for four decades by the Green Belt Movement are listed in Fig.13 below. GBM bases its work on the following values:- love for environment conservation; self and community empowerment; volunteerism; strong sense of belonging to a community of like-minded people; accountability, transparency, honesty.

From the outset, the GBM tree-planting campaign was linked to food security and water harvesting at household level, civic education, advocacy, Green Belt safaris to gain inspiration from elsewhere, and Pan-African training workshops. Kenya has been well-supplied with information to help appropriate tree-planting there. However, GBM results have been spectacular, with well over 30 million trees planted in Kenya alone - a triumph of rural forestation and reforestation. Rural employment has been created and environmental awareness raised. Individuals and communities have been inspired, empowered and mobilised. Biodiversity, a wider range of food crops and water catchments have been protected locally. Women have risen in status through their practice, with associated increase in availability of agricultural tools, advocacy and networking via GBM. All this has led to extensive documentation and recognition of GBM internationally. Lessons learned by GBM include: community felt needs must be addressed; participants must perceive the sense of this work; good leadership is vital; community motivation requires patience and commitment; short-term incentives help poor people to engage with it; both decision-makers and communities need to be reached simultaneously; GBM field staff must be keen observers; communities must understand the project objectives and own it; limited resources demand prioritisation; democratic administration and management is key.

The Mission of GBM is

> ...to mobilise community consciousness for self-determination, equity, improved livelihood securities and environmental conservation using trees as the entry point.

Figure 13. The Ten-Step GBM Procedure for adoption of Tree-Planting (Maathai, 2006)

1.	Dissemination of information to communities on tree-planting importance;
2.	Facilitation of Group formation in communities;
3.	Registration of Groups with GBM HQ;
4.	Preparation of Tree Nursery sites by Groups;
5.	Reporting monthly by Groups to GBM HQ;
6.	Announcement by Groups to communities:-'seedlings ready', inviting interest to dig holes;
7.	Checking of tree holes by Group members;
8.	Issuing of tree seedlings to those who dug holes properly;
9.	Verification of tree seedling survival by Group members, reporting to GBM HQ;
10.	Second verification of seedling survival, and purchase of seedlings by GBM if successful.

There are constraints in promoting tree-planting, such as the taboos on fruit tree planting in northern Ghana where some fear they will die once the trees planted start fruiting. However, there is real pride in tree planting too such that people will hardly destroy trees they have planted themselves (they may do so with donated trees if they wish to plant their own annual crops there, as observed in Haiti). During long dry seasons, many fodder trees are browsed by livestock but few people plant them. Hay for dry season livestock feeding can be made from the foliage of a number of trees including *Bauhinia* species (Neatsfoot in RSA) and a range of mulberry trees (*Morus spp.*). There is a range of tropical leguminous trees and shrubs *Leucaena spp., Gliricidia spp.* ("Mother of Cocoa"), pigeon pea (*Cajanus cajan*) used for alley cropping. *Calliandra calothyrsus* is an excellent fodder tree candidate and also attracts bees for bee-keeping microenterprises. The challenge is to scale up the use of such species. All steps to plant more trees merit consideration since too many households depend on selling charcoal thus further depleting existing tree cover. Adoption of fuel-saving stoves (https://fourthway.co.uk/) needs to go alongside tree-planting. These can save as much as 70% of wood fuel compared with typical cooking on three stones.

Environmentally appropriate forest management ensures that the harvest of timber and non-timber products maintains the forest's biodiversity, productivity, and ecological processes. Socially beneficial forest management helps both local people and society at large to enjoy long-term benefits and also provides strong incentives to local people to sustain the forest resources and adhere to long-term management plans. Economically viable forest management means that forest operations are structured and managed so as to be sufficiently profitable, without generating financial profit at the expense of the forest resource, the ecosystem, or affected communities. The tension between the need to generate adequate financial returns and the principles of responsible forest operations can be reduced through efforts to market the full range of forest products and services for their best value.

Based on experience of rural community development and field extension work in Africa, it seems that fourteen points integrate to promote tree progress for sub-Saharan Africa (Fig.14).

Figure 14. Proposals for Tree and Forest Promotion

• Teach Bible heritage basis	• Plant/retain riverbank trees
• Lift Environment awareness	• Promote Bee-keeping
• Promote Tree Nurseries	• Livestock control/housing
• Encourage 2-trees/house	• Best home & village competitions
• Promote use of tree guards	• Junior Conservation Clubs
• Fuel-efficient stoves	• Environment Care Groups
• Add value to forest produce	• Churches as Demonstration points

Responses following practical workshops facilitated by the author in four villages in Malawi in 2012 are shown in Appendix 1 below. Participants were asked to identify what they had learned or been reminded about during the workshop, with whom they would share this, and what they would do during the next six months with the resources that they control or influence. This is an approach followed by the author with farmers, churches and rural communities over the past four decades at the end of practical workshops on integral mission.

Trees and forests, their planting and protection offer a unifying focus for sustainable rural development. Both locally and globally they link to communal well-being – the Biblical "tree of life." Reversal of the alarming scale of tree removal is urgent in many places, especially in sub-Saharan Africa. Integral management involving trees – such as in agroforestry - is vital for genuinely sustainable intensification for the rising global population's food security. A global policy framework for forest stewardship must be rigorously applied by each nation. However, only by engaging indigenous people and integrating tree care within their livelihoods can progress be attained.

Fuel-Saving Stoves

Africa is damaged by its current and growing contribution to global warming from deforestation for cooking fuel. Some 85% of trees cut down in Africa are reckoned destined for fuel-wood use – often on flue-less fires between three stones with huge energy-inefficiency. This typically uses some 2.5+ times the wood needed otherwise, consequently damaging the environment, impairing soil and water conservation, taking immense time for fuelwood collection, depleting family budgets, and impairing the health of cooks.

In survey work in Kenya, Uganda and Malawi, though there are fuel-saving Larena and/or Dembe stoves made, some are not used regularly and there is still frequent co-existence of '3 stones' cooking alongside improved stoves. The reason for this given by many is that the 3 stones plus pot can be boiled more quickly. The solution to this understandable but counter-productive thinking is:

* to teach and practice *planning* to start cooking earlier;
* to *continue* using the improved stoves (which get better with use);
* to extend the stove *chimney* so that it can draw better and thus heat quickly when needed (nevertheless allowing some smoke to impinge on the outer wall of the kitchen to deter insect pests from colonising the kitchen walls!);
* to develop the notion of *heating control* by means of wood ash to damp down while using a flat stone to temporarily restrict air-intake gap to speed up burning initially;
* to teach the improved nutritional value of *slower cooking.*

Training on the win-win-win-win-win aspects of fuel-saving stoves needs keen advocacy, viz. fuel saved, time saved collecting it, trees saved, money saved, health of the cook saved. Better monitoring of the subsequent use of stoves would help to refine their operation.

Meanwhile, we have the spectre of cassava exports for energy generation (and advertising in the West as "green energy") when it is actually "the food security crop" of West Africa - and elsewhere.

Ecomedicines

The natural world is widely supplied with natural medicines and remedies for treating ailments and allergies among both people and livestock. Furthermore, it is well-known that companion-planting of appropriate species can reduce plant pest and disease attacks, such as by placing African marigolds (*Tagetes*) among cabbages and other Brassica crops. Given the beneficent nature of our Creator, should we be surprised?! The challenge is for us to understand, collate and use these 'ecomedicines' wisely. For many remote and impoverished communities far from any pharmacy, or crop/animal protection suppliers, these ecomedicines are both freely available and accessible if only knowledge - often indigenous technical knowledge (ITK) - is passed on from generation to generation. All too often, such ITK dies out or is neglected in the wake of supposed superior "modernisation." One charity that specialises in conservation of such ITK and of the plants from which ecomedicines are derived is Action for Natural Medicines (https://anamed.org/en/). Revelation 22:2 speaks of *the leaves of the tree for the healing of the nations.* Jesus used His own spittle and a mud paste to heal a blind man (John 9:6) while David famously used the healing power of music to soothe King Saul when he was troubled by an evil spirit (1 Sam.16:23).

Numerous examples of healing plants occur all over the world. Perhaps the best-known one to rural British children is the dock leaf (*Rumex obtusifolius*) to rub into flesh stung by nettles (*Urtica dioica*) - noting the wonder that wherever nettles grow, then docks seem to be not far away! A whole range of potions can be made from plants and often transported in dry powder form to preserve them and enable easy storage and sale/dispensing. Others can be distilled into oil formulations, such as Comfrey (*Symphytum officinale*) to be applied as "knitbone" rubbed into arthritic joints for relief. Leaves of the drumstick tree (*Moringa oleifera*) are a rich source of vitamins and minerals, as well as providing a suitable herb tea for diabetes sufferers. Leaves of *Artemisia annua* are dried to use as a herbal tea countering malaria. The dried leaves of the neem tree (*Azadirachta indica*) provide a useful vermifuge to de-worm livestock. The list of valuable sources is huge. However, one must beware those plants that have poisonous parts, or else are wholly toxic such as *Atropa belladonna*, deadly nightshade. Extracts of some plants that are toxic as whole plants may be used to prepare carefully-formulated pharmaceutical products, such as digitalin from foxgloves (*Digitalis purpurea*).

Chapter 6

Economy For Enough

Poverty Reduction

Poverty means detrimental lack. Poverty is normally thought of to apply mainly to lack of necessary material things for a decent life but it can also involve lack of humility towards God through being monetarily rich. It is possible to be both "down and out" and "up and out" – both cases needy. However, recognising one is poor in some way can be beneficial and the start of relief, as when Jesus said *Blessed are the poor in spirit, for theirs is the kingdom of heaven* (Matt.5:3). *There will always be poor people in the land. Therefore I command you to be open-handed.* (Deut.15:11). Jesus valued good news reaching the poor (Matt.11:5) and Paul and Barnabas were eager to help the poor (Gal.2:10).

However, poverty has many causes and Scripture also warns against idleness, wastefulness and misuse of resources leading to poverty. For instance, idle chatter [rather than hard work] leads to poverty (Prov.14:23) and the sluggard (lazy person) neglects care of the land so that it is full of weeds and its fences are broken down (Prov.24:30-34). Often, poverty is both caused by and reinforced by unjust behaviour on the part of the rich – *Whoever oppresses the poor shows contempt for their Maker, but whoever is kind to the needy honours God.* (Prov.14:31). Jesus condemned unjust stewardship (Luke 16:1-13) and concluded that one cannot serve God and mammon (money and all it can buy). It is vital to teach the value of proper resource management, including money entrusted to individuals, churches and organisations so that it might flow efficiently to those causes that genuinely relieve poverty of all kinds. Relieving material poverty is no good if it leads people into the worship of money and greed to gain more. A very wealthy American was once asked how many dollars are enough?' and replied 'a dollar more than you have!' We need to learn the value of contentment as taught by Paul – *I have learned to be content whatever the circumstances.* (Phil.4:11). In 1 Tim 6:6-10 he taught *godliness with contentment is great gain ... we brought nothing into the world, and we can take nothing out of it ... the love of money is a root of all kinds of evil.* Jesus warned (Luke 12:15).

Material poverty can result from:

a.   being born into an impoverished family - perhaps in a slum; being orphaned.
b.   suffering a natural disaster such as a flood.
c.   suffering theft of possessions.
d.   inability to earn money through disability or illness or ethnic persecution.
e.   systemic injustice in communities that deny access to work or to adequate wealth.
f.   laziness to work hard enough or at all or absence of parental role models to endeavour.
g.   gambling or otherwise squandering one's wealth in showy expenditure.

Work towards poverty reduction involves:

a.   Biblical teaching on the poor/poverty – idleness, waste, injustice, compassion, action.

b.   Practical workshops involving analysis of the causes and possible cures for poverty.

c.   Biblical teaching on hard work, holy living, talent-spotting - for healthy livelihoods.

d.   Training on resource management for water catchment, composting, fuel-saving etc.

e.   Training on farmers' groups, improved farming methods and value-adding to produce.

f.   Training on microenterprise and job creation, on business management and marketing.

g.   Training and enabling on microfinance.

h.   Biblical teaching on the snares of materialism.

i.   Training on waste reduction and recycling.

j.   Advocacy towards greater justice and on behalf of the poor and voiceless.

k.   Biblical teaching on development of 'best practice' ministries of compassion for poor.

Materialism, Money And Debt

You cannot serve God and Money said Jesus (Matt 6:24). Materialism, rather than atheism, agnosticism or communism, is often the main rival to Christian belief, or indeed to any spirituality. The seed is choked by the cares of this world (Matt 13:7). Greed overtakes need. Acquisitiveness is an addiction nurtured by advertising, fuelled by e-commerce and credit cards (as distinct from *debit cards* where only money saved is available for spending) and cheered on by the "live now, pay later" philosophy portrayed in the advertising media. Perhaps worse still, there are those who pedal the deception and delusion of "the prosperity gospel," which proposes that material riches are God's purpose for all. Of course, if we humans shared more equitably the limited resources of earth, then more could live more comfortably than at present. As someone has said, "let us live more simply that others may simply live." However, even some mainline Christian churches seem to have jettisoned the qualms they had in earlier times about encouraging the gambling mentality of lotteries and their near equivalents. All this suggests that worship of greed and getting more for less has grabbed contemporary global culture. "Least cost" methods of production, especially for natural products such as food, lead to serious consequences for the environment and for human communities since the true ecological and social costs are not adequately paid in the drive to maximise short-term gains. Paul urged (Romans 12:2), *Do not conform to the pattern of this world, but be transformed by the renewing of your mind.*

The warning of I Tim.6:10 concerns "the love of money" and not "money" *per se.* Lust after money and what it can buy can "pierce us through with many sorrows," most especially if and when we allow unnecessary indebtedness to become a defining characteristic of our lifestyle. "Love of money" disqualifies people for leadership in the church (1 Tim 3:3). The very challenge of living as human beings on earth is to strike the right balance in our attitudes and practices to the material and the spiritual dimensions of reality. The Deists made the error of separating what they perceived to be the banalities of the material from the higher values of the spiritual. Jesus did not so compartmentalise but rather he integrated the material and the spiritual in all his ministry; he provided "not bread alone" (Matt 4:4; Luke 4:4) but he did provide physical bread too (e.g. Mark 8:1-10). Isaiah warned against the misguidedness of "spending money on that which is not bread" (Isa.55:2). Proper stewardship of money and its use in legitimate business is clearly taught in the parable of the talents of money (Matt 25:15 ff.). Avoiding extorting money in excessive interest rates or taxes is taught in Luke 3:14. For Peter (1 Peter 5:2) the antithesis of greediness for money is eagerness to serve the Lord.

The Bible teaches that:

1. A proper attitude to material things is to perceive them as God-given to receive with thanks, to share and to steward sustainably;
2. Material and spiritual development is to be pursued simultaneously in integral mission;
3. The love of money and "retail therapy" are in direct opposition to God's will and purposes;
4. Legitimate business should be pursued profitably but equitably as to resource use and the fair reward of those who labour in it;
5. Debt is undesirable, although it may be unavoidable, at least in a partial way via a mortgage, in order to acquire a basic home to live in. However, going into debt to acquire unnecessary items is never wise or right, and may amount to gambling with our health and expected lifespan to pay back or to avoid future emergency needs – even leaving an inheritance of debt for the next generation;
6. Strategic prayerful planning is needed to avoid debt or to help those who have become indebted to recover their equilibrium and integral material/spiritual priorities.
7. Save up for needs, maintain strategic limited reserves to be ready to help the needy.

Microfinance

Small farms and rural businesses employ limited capital, one person or only a few people and thus have limited financial turnover. Of course, small businesses can grow into larger ones. Part of the skill and wisdom needed to run a business lies in deciding when it risks getting too big. Greed can drive a successful small business to over-borrow and so to expand that the initiator of it loses control or becomes controlled by its insatiable demands upon her or his time. Businesses require sound management of all their resources, notably their personnel. The management of objectives, of change, and of time requires strategic planning and honest review of performance. Businesses can have a life cycle and need not last for ever; it takes courage to close down a business before it fails. Very often, more can be achieved by collaboration, though this has the prerequisite of mutual trust, which takes time and shared moral values to establish. Both business acumen and training help. Proper record-keeping to monitor performance, regular evaluation and discussion of teamwork, and communications are vital to success in management. The business mind-set may take time to develop and require ongoing training but early transfer of responsibility for limited credit provision must be made to farmers and small business proprietors themselves, otherwise dependency will set in and the credit provider will suffer administrative diversion from a more fruitful role of integral management training.

Microfinance requires not only a provider (bank, credit society or NGO), but also accountability and this is often to be provided by a group who stand surety for any member in the necessarily unusual case of their default on repayments. Group failure results when such mutual trust is betrayed either by excessive defaulters or by mis-use of shared funds such as by embezzlers. Small loans can be highly significant in enabling small businesses to get started, such as illustrated by the Grameen ("Village") banks across Bangladesh since 1983 founded by Yunus, who has since proposed an international approach of "social businesses." He began after loaning just US$ 27 to 42 poor people. The *Grameen* Bank in 2009 had some 2,520 branches with 27,000 staff serving over 7.5 million micro-loan borrowers in all villages of Bangladesh. It lends over US$ 1 billion annually; 97% of borrowers are women and over 98% of loans are repaid without problems. The model has inspired similar micro-finance schemes all over the world.

Group lending is well shown through ACAT (Africa Co-operative Action Trust in Southern Africa since 1979 (www.acat.co.za) using an uncopiable stamp to endorse inspected records that are then audited. However, since the late 1990s, ACAT in South Africa has moved away from forming and supporting Savings Clubs directly as in earlier days, owing to its time and cost commitment, and the wish of ACAT to foster independence as far as possible (McCrystal, 2005). This is an experience echoed in Nigeria. In South Africa since 2000, ACAT has focused more on training in groups and encouraged direct interaction with banks and with local credit unions such as *stokvels* for provision of necessary finance. Previously, the running of ACAT Savings Clubs had become a massive undertaking to support and service with both "in house" extension and auditing commitments. *Stokvels* ("stock fairs" where livestock were traditionally traded along with celebrations) are savings or investment societies to which members regularly contribute an agreed amount and from which they receive a lump sum payment. They often hold regular parties wearing distinctive uniforms and with their own songs. These are funded by the members and generate profits for the hosts. They serve as revolving loan credit unions in which members pay in fixed sums of money to a central fund periodically (weekly, fortnightly or monthly). Each month a different member receives the money in the fund collected during that period. People do not fail to make contributions owing to strong group culture. Members use their allocated fund either for payments or for investment purposes. The key points about *stokvels* are cultural embeddedness, mutuality and independent management. It can be argued that ACAT's period of twenty years focus through Savings Clubs has been foundational for such independence with its training of ACAT Clubs' farmer committees in organisation, administration and enterprise development. Training is ongoing in these aspects alongside other livelihood skills but there is no longer the systematic commitment of time and funds by ACAT in supervising and auditing its own network of Savings Clubs as hitherto.

ACAT Kwazulu-Natal (2011) recorded,

> Facilitating sustained transformation of people remains the essence of ACAT's work and focus. [Worldwide] today so much effort focuses on changing the environment, rather than changing people who in turn can change their environment. ACAT has tried and tested this approach since 1979, and our experience informs us that the only way this is realised is by finding ways of inviting God back into every dimension and area of our lives, and to promote the same to our target group and their communities. A question we regularly ask ourselves regarding God's active participation in our lives is: how can any intervention be sustainable if the Creator is left out, or on the fringe of things?

From the perspective of "delivering credit via servicing Savings Clubs," ACAT Kwazulu-Natal had moved away from any direct involvement by 2011, enabling it to quadruple during ten years (2000-2011) the number of people directly helped in its first twenty years (1979-99)! Over many years, ACAT Kwazulu-Natal administered many small rand loans totalling R1,896,068 million. This is now replaced by intensified ACAT promotion of, and training in, community-driven savings and loan schemes, where people mobilise and distribute themselves the funds they need. This is a highly significant strategic change, not only for more effective use of ACAT's resources but also in development of people's responsibility for their own financial management.

In Uganda, *Kulika* has piloted a micro-finance loan scheme among farmers in their groups as they have developed trust in one another. Through this, over 400 individuals have been helped. Many *FARMS* (Farm Asset Resource Management Study) Groups [see section on *FARMS* Groups] have been started through *Kulika* and associated NGOs in Uganda. The most successful members managed to more than triple their income and assets. Loan repayments mostly came in without difficulty on time. Reinvestment of these profits was in various sustainable ways:

* in soil management, better seeds and in cultivating more land;
* in diversification into livestock enterprises or new types of crop;
* in improved household facilities: tin roof, water tank, proper latrines, fuel-saving stoves;
* in setting up new businesses, notably shops, processing & direct selling of farm produce.

It is considered vital that these groups manage their own loans and repayments rather than becoming an administrative burden upon *Kulika* thus distracting its efforts and resources from its proper role of extension to promote independent enterprise and associated financial management, enabling believers to support church-based charitable needs.

In Kenya, over 4,000 farm families have been helped via IcFEM Kimilili (Inter-Christian Fellowships' Evangelical Mission; https://www.icfem-mission.org/) to gain Government of Kenya/Equity Bank help. IcFEM has sought to avoid dependency as a catalysing NGO so that groups take responsibility for their own savings and credit management (Table Banking) from the outset, in the context of regular Bible teaching, worship and fellowship together.

Experience over more than four decades in sub-Saharan Africa in promoting sustainable agriculture and farm-household technologies shows the importance of making sustainable financial management training an integral part of that. There may well be a process for subsistence farmers on small farms whereby initial catalysis and help is needed to instil a properly managed savings and reinvestment culture, perhaps with "seed" capital for strategic borrowing. However, ultimate responsibility for loans and repayments must be with people themselves. The key lesson is that this needs to be made clear from the outset of any rural credit scheme. Also, when supportive rural NGOs devote themselves to training and extension of proper financial management alongside suitably sustainable livelihoods teaching, then great impacts can be secured to strengthen the huge number of small farm households upon which the future of Africa's truly sustainable food security depends.

Christian NGOs and the Global Financial System

Christian NGOs that genuinely seek to do work of eternal significance will be expected to have God-honouring origins of Biblically-based vision, faith and trust in God's providence. God is indeed *Jehovah-Jireh,* the LORD our ultimate provider (Gen 22:14). However, He neither condones complacent financial excess nor mean-mindedness regarding use of money. The Bible teaches prudent investment (the parable of the talents is about real money! Matt.25:14ff.). It is the *love* of money and not money *per se* that Paul describes as *a root of all evil* (1 Tim.6:10).

Very often, the best mission and practical development work is done "on a shoestring" i.e. with income just meeting demand in a continually faith-testing way! This observation was made to me as a young man by my mentor and friend Peter Batchelor, and by our late mutual tutor in tropical agriculture, Dr Geoffrey Masefield of Oxford University. I have found it to be very true. The inspiring life of George Müller in Bristol and the West Country of England from 1830-1898 testifies to this, and the benefits to orphans and the underprivileged still continue well beyond his death (Telfer, 2006; Steer, 2018). In today's money, Müller raised £100 million during his lifetime and provided homes for 120,000 orphans he rescued from the cruel streets of Bristol. He also engaged in international speaking and Bible-teaching literature work in later life too. He achieved all this without making any appeals or using fund-raising techniques. He and his wife and colleagues simply *prayed.* God met their needs in continually miraculous ways, proving His reality and that He can be trusted.

How did the global financial crisis of 2008 develop? Through materialism-based lack of vision, misplaced faith in speculation (effectively international gambling) and misplaced trust in the idea that greed can be pursued without consequences (Isa.56:10-12). It has been well said that if one follows selfish ways one gets consequences but if one follows God's ways, one gets results! The removal of protocols or regulatory boundaries in the late 1990s set the scene for easy credit with rampant over-borrowing (far in excess of the capacity to repay, notably on mortgages for housing). Furthermore, hazard was compounded by the invention of dubious "credit packages" and their indiscriminate trading, which separated borrower from any sort of relationship with lender. Above all, this has led to exploitation of the poor who are least able to cope with the consequences; some should never have been "saddled" with unpayable debts in mortgages designed to feed the lenders' financial speculation.

The international coronavirus pandemic of 2020-21, is seen by many believers as a wake-up call from God who loves us still and seeks that we should repent and trust Him. Its impact on people's lives has been immense, continues, and is yet to be fully realised. What is certain is that *Jesus Christ is the same yesterday, today and for ever* (Heb.13:8) and God invites *whosoever* to trust in him.

How should the Christian NGO respond to a situation of constrained finances and economic turmoil? The following are suggested:

1. Put **Prayer** first. Getting in tune with God's heartbeat for His world and His priorities for mission.
2. **Repent** and turn back to God and to Biblically-based attitudes to morals, money, funding and stewardship of resources for sustainable livelihoods.
3. **Practice** what we preach regarding good stewardship to achieve more with less waste. This includes avoiding the scandal that some Christian charities have exorbitant salaries for their CEOs and staff. One can argue that no Christian leader should require more for day-to-day living than the average income of those they lead, although allowing for such extras as necessary travel costs.
4. **Avoid** panic, which indicates fear rather than trust in a faithful Creator – this is especially true regarding climate change. We must act responsibly, of course, but God has given us an inherently stable earth and promised that while it remains, seedtime and harvest, cold and heat, summer and winter, day and night will not cease (Gen.8:22)
5. **Abstain** from worldly methods of fund-raising. Fund-raising in the West has become an "industry" in its own right with frequently disappointing yields! However, acquainting committed supporters and friends with real mission needs when

asked, or presenting needs to relevant Trusts that exist to fund such causes can be done legitimately. Though it must be noted that Müller avoided even this, even with close friends, preferring to leave God to prompt them to give directly in response to his earnest prayers directed only to God. That is a real challenge but his testimony proves needs were met!

6. **Seek advice** from wise counsellors. The change in the value of hard currencies, such as the reduced value of pounds sterling when turned into some African currencies has hit many NGOs very hard. A strategic rethink of spending priorities may be timely.

7. Never forget **Thanksgiving.** Paul advised the Thessalonians that it is God's will that we give Him thanks in all circumstances – not just during the easy times! (I Thess. 5:18).

Partnership for Delivery of Compassionate Funding

Funding God's work is a matter of prayer and trust, not of slick manipulation of those able to give using worldly fundraising techniques. One of the names of God is *Jehovah-Jireh,* the LORD our provider (Gen.22:14). We need to pray to him to release those funds making those trusts and individual friends adequately aware of a mission's work and needs, without pressurised appeals. Also, delivery of financial help must be done with due regard to the poor's capacity to use the funds effectively and honestly. If necessary, capacity to manage funds must be built so that all may 'give an account of their stewardship' (Luke 16:2). In order to deliver compassionate financial assistance to the poor, givers of the required funds need a relationship of mutual respect to be maintained between Supporting Organisations (SO) and Implementing Organisations (IO) such as a mission operating directly with the poor beneficiaries. God is the ultimate giver via the hands of regular donors of resources for the SO/IO Partnership to deliver (1 Chron.29:12).

It may be helpful to consider the parallel of traffic lights for cash flow. Only by giving resources can the process of transfer to the poor begin. Only thus can *"Stop"* be changed to *"Get Ready To Go."* The SO exists to catalyse and to steward this flow directly.

The *"Get Ready To Go"* stage is the responsibility of the SO and IO in partnership through a mutual agreement to act together in a covenant relationship before God, with minimal bureaucracy but maximal transparency to ensure effective transfer of relevant help to the poor.

The *"Go"* stage is directly brought about by the IO with ongoing partnership from the SO. Together they work to monitor, improve and account for the progress of their jointly-agreed programme or project.

Proposed Partnership Principles include the following:

1.   That the SO/IO partnership be viewed as analogous to marriage in that neither partner alone can achieve their compassionate objectives in producing and raising offspring;
2.   That the partners covenant together before God faithfully to deliver to the poor His resources (released via the hands of givers through the SO);
3.   That both proposal writing and report writing guidelines speak consistently of our joint responsibility (SO+IO) in providing clear, regular information (narrative and financial). This is in order to be transparently accountable to God, to givers, to legal charity bodies *and* to recipient beneficiaries of resources given. In this way, together we may stimulate further release of such resources. Proper, rigorous, concise reports are vital and to be elicited by the language of *teamwork* between SO and IO.

4.   That both SO and IO strive to maintain a mutually sensitive, co-
      equal partnership (Eph.4:3) recognising that neither owns the
      resources but rather as partners we share joint responsibility for
      the transfer process to benefit the poor.

If we pursue the above principles of partnership with integrity, we can
by God's grace serve together to the building of His Kingdom through
integral mission as truly integral Partners in funding genuine need.

Fairer Trading

There is evident need for an international framework within which
sustainably-informed private enterprise creativity can operate to the
mutual benefit of farmers (producers) and consumers. Management
should be applied, rather than leaving farmers and rural communities
to drown in a tsunami of liberalisation, exacerbated by trade war
storms whenever large producer-trader countries choose to erect *ad
hoc* tariff barriers within their avowed "free trade" philosophy. Fairer
International Agricultural Trading (FIAT) is proposed in the form
of the sort of *"Highway Code"* that governments of countries issue to
regulate traffic flow in a sensible manner. Food trading needs limiting
boundaries as recognised necessary for over-fishing, rainforest felling,
and traffic management.

Towards a HIGHWAY CODE for SustainableTrading Management:

1.   Lead international agreement to change WTO policy of *non-
      discrimination against imports* (i.e. which aims to be tariff-free)
      negotiating and substituting a *Highway Code for Trading.* We
      do *not* need enterprise-stifling attempts at micro-management
      but we do need a common-sense framework for law and order

providing boundaries within which markets can operate to reconcile simultaneous needs of environment, livelihoods, food security and land heritage.

2.   Seek to raise public awareness in each country of the livelihood, environmental and defence importance of buying locally grown foods as much as possible. Landscapes should be both beautiful to look at and good for food everywhere; only enough farmers in place can deliver that in each country. Biological ecosystem limitations of "comparative advantage" - not short-term financial speculation - must ultimately govern food policies.

3.   Challenge trade involving delivery of products to countries where they could perfectly well be grown already e.g. much rice in many African countries is quite unnecessarily and damagingly coming from Asia. Chickens and eggs are being traded around the world when they can perfectly well be raised in most countries. Cheap USA maize has been ruinous to Mexico.

4.   Encourage fair-trade policies product-by-product, such as with *Café Direct* and also with tea, as a prelude to an internationally agreed comprehensive fair trading context.

5.   Maximise processing of products prior to export **within** their countries of farm production e.g. peanut butter *in situ*, solar-dry tropical fruits, process beverage crops in-country.

6.   "Remove agricultural products from the current WTO policy" to offer immediate help - but other trading can be excessive also harming livelihoods and the environment.

7.   Encourage farmers to form *FARMS* - Farm Asset Resource Management Study - groups in which they meet from farm to farm, learn together, and maybe earn/trade together.

Towards Fairer Trading: Possible Mechanisms to Improve Food Security Internationally:

- Trade regulation accords on a regional basis with trade quota 'sieves' to implement;
- National strategies to feed family first, animals second and markets third;
- Recovery of national food sovereignty, notably national control over staple food policy;
- Provision of proper food reserve "safety nets," especially targeting the vulnerable;
- Fuel tax on freight for bulky products which can perfectly well be grown at destination;
- Farmer conservation policies to maintain strong agrarian structure; train new entrants;
- Food production incentives e.g. via credit unions; seed banks conserving many cultivars;
- Local market infrastructure & consumer education to encourage buying local produce;
- Encouraging farmers with training for enterprise development and niche marketing.

Chapter 7

Management for Development

Criteria for Leadership Development

If the overall aim of integral mission is to develop discipleship for creation care, then leadership development is central to its attainment. For good or ill, leaders multiply messages. Leaders exert potentially the greatest impact on any organisation's values and business ethics. How a leader views leadership styles and values can be very revealing. The Bible records much about leadership exposing both good and bad leaders – among the latter are many false teachers.

- It is vital that leadership messages are Biblically derived (e.g.1 Tim 3:1-13).
- To lead is to accept responsibility to serve (John 13:1-17).

In order to develop leadership it may be necessary to:

- Facilitate the review of leadership styles and issues for both individuals and organisations in the context of strategic planning for improvement, in the light of the servant leadership of Jesus Christ (Phil.2:1-11);
- Prioritise leadership training and the facilitation of networking between established and younger leaders to enable cross-

fertilisation of ideas, experience and fellowship via mentoring and coaching;

• Encourage and facilitate the conduct of workshops and courses for leaders;
• Encourage formation of Christian Development Associations to foster leadership collaboration on a national basis in various countries.

Jesus is our role-model for leadership development. Jesus selected a team of twelve diverse, ordinary people and developed them as disciples. He did so by integrating theory and practice, by itinerant ministry using participatory methods. He did not build a physical institution but rather concentrated on building a sustainable network through mobilising the whole body of believers. He didn't try to do everything himself but rather built a team. He taught them how to pray, to act and also how to rest. He imparted values. He led by example. His church consists not of visible buildings but rather of people. It is international, transcends denominations and is eternal, empowered by the Holy Spirit to enable transformation of individuals and communities. Sadly, membership is smaller than that of the visible church.

Leaders are enablers. They are catalysts whose spark may vitally inspire, instigate and motivate change in people's understanding, attitudes, appreciation and subsequent actions. Rather than becoming noisy overlords, authoritarians or "control freaks," they need to become "lubricants." In an engine, the lubricant enables smooth operation; it is only evident when absent such that the engine rattles! A leader in any organisation is thus not condemned to a life of striving to try to become the ultimate omni-competent, all-singing, all-dancing expert on every aspect of that organisation's work! That is the sure route to stress and disaster for both the leader and the organisation. A strong leader recognises, encourages, enables, delegates and coordinates development of the talents of others so that the team together can achieve. As John the Baptist said on seeing Jesus approaching, *He must become greater; I must become less* (John 3:30). A good leader focuses on achieving not only the task in hand but also harmonious team relationships. Leadership involves team management and change management. It is a technical and pastoral art in itself, with God-given human talent as its medium.

If the church in Africa is to grow in depth through discipleship rather than simply in numbers by conversion alone, more leaders will be needed who are Biblically-grounded, humble, Spirit-led and evidently gracious. Leaders set the tone for those who follow. Effective leaders are constructive, wholistic encouragers who pursue the goals advocated by Micah 6:8: *To act justly and to love mercy and to walk humbly with your God.* It seems from Biblical and contemporary testimonies to be a prerequisite that they themselves know what it is to be broken by circumstances so that their *hard edges* are softened and substituted with the supreme quality of compassion (love in action).

Mentoring and Coaching

Mentoring and coaching is all about the intentional influence of one person upon another. Mentoring involves influencing the way one thinks about things, about mental attitudes and about steering our minds into constructive modes and habits of thought. Coaching concerns more the mechanical acquisition of skills. It is about the hands, the actions; about the proper application of skills to perform a task effectively, safely and efficiently. Proverbs 18:24 warns about the impact of the type of companions we keep. Many sayings likewise alert us to this, such as *birds of a feather flock together*. Jesus was angry with those who had made the temple area *a den of robbers* (Mark 11:17). It is possible to mentor and coach people towards wrong goals as well as towards good behaviour. Good parenting is very much mentoring and coaching to lay solid foundations for right living, about providing a proper role model for thinking and service in this world, and preparation for the next world in heaven. Many of the epistles as well as the book of Acts, describe mentoring and coaching relationships – such as Paul towards Timothy and many others (e.g. 2 Tim 4:9). Sometimes mentees desert their mentors later on (e.g. Demas – 2 Tim 4:10). Overbearing mentors who become too controlling well deserve such desertion! Missionaries are really mentors and coaches whose jobs are to work themselves out of jobs, handing on the baton of responsibility to others who are usually more local and younger. The Christian motivation for mentoring and coaching comes from the Holy Spirit within – from a new heart (Ezek 36:26). The psalmist (Psa 86:11) reminds us that the person of integrity does not just have a *mind* but also a *will* and a *heart*; it is a prayer for integrity. Good Christian mentoring and coaching springs from an undivided (undistracted) heart. Neither the mind nor the will nor the heart must dominate but rather all should work together in balance for an approach of integrity.

Coaching involves task analysis, demonstration of good practice and providing opportunities to emulate proper technique. "Practice makes perfect" so "if at first you don't succeed, try, try again." Athletes and sportspersons employ coaches to analyse their techniques and moods.

Qualities and Ethical Behaviour required for effective mentoring and coaching include:

Listening skills; "walking with" (Lk.24:32); integrity; competence; experience as a practitioner; networking contacts with other relevant people and organisations; devotion of enough time to mentees or trainees (Phil.2:4); willingness to enable, to watch others advance and sometimes to overtake one (as with John the Baptist and Jesus – *He must become greater; I must become less*, John 3:30).

> The **VISION** of mentoring and coaching is to promote professional excellence:
> Voluntarily Industriously Sustainably Integrally Objectively
> Nutritively (nurturing progress in the mentee/learner).

We all need to be engaged in Continuing Professional Development (CPD) for Lifelong learning (LLL). Paul said his aim was to present everyone mature in Christ (Col.1:28). Such is the role model of an effective mentor and coach. A Learning Contract, agreement or Memorandum of Understanding (MoU) might be written down at the outset of a mentoring relationship once mentee and mentor have established rapport. On it, a mentee should state their time-framed learning goals and the steps, dynamics and skills needed to attain them. It is wise to agree not only frequency of meetings at the outset but also a regular review of progress so that the arrangement might be discontinued by mutual agreement without recrimination or embarrassment. A statement that neither mentor nor mentee regards the learning contract as legally binding may be a wise precaution if an organisation is to develop a general mentoring scheme. Those offering paid mentoring services may offer a legal contract to provide learning services. However, most agreements should just record the mentee's own set targets for learning and provide a means to record their attainment within a friendly mentoring relationship.

What mentoring and coaching lessons can be gleaned from a) Mary; b) Paul? (see his letters to Timothy and Philemon).

Building Teamwork based on DiscerningDiscipleship

That teamwork and mutual accountability in development beats individualism is implicit in:

- Psalm 68:6, which suggests a family context for faith to be worked out;
- Ephesians, which through the whole book stresses **"Us, Together, We;"**
- Jesus with 12 disciples who had clear objectives and methods (Mark 1:15);
- The Great Commission to "Make disciples, teach all things, all nations" (Matt.28:19,20);
- Manageable group size (12), using parables, demonstration/ practice, catalysing/enabling
- Identifying, encouraging, equipping and establishing local leadership and teams;
- Focus on mutually motivated permanent change for the better (discipleship)
- Ordinary folk chosen in Christ, accepted by the Father, empowered by the Holy Spirit;
- "Closeness to the Cross is the key to closeness with others;"
- "Co-operation is better than Conflict;"
- "The best number of directors is odd and three is too many!" – but leaders need teams!
- Conventional wisdom (see Cormack, 1987) says, "The 6 most important words are 'I admit I made a mistake;'" The 5 most important words are "You did a good job;" The 4 most important are "What is your opinion?;" The 3 most important words are "If

you please;" The 2 most important words are "Thank you;" The least important word is "I."

GROWING teams (according to Cormack, 1987) engage in: **G**athering information; **R**eviewing the target; **O**ption finding; **W**eighing options; **I**dentifying solutions; **N**ecessary action; **G**aining insights.

Factors for effective teamwork observed in practice include:

• Grace – inspired by the leader and adopted by participants.
• Relaxed atmosphere.
• Frequent, relevant discussion.
• Clear targets.
• Open listening.
• Disagreements openly shared and treated.
• Consensus sought on actions.
• Constructive criticism welcomed.
• Delegation.
• Acceptance.
• Working relationships established.
• Trust and confidence established.
• All "press towards the mark" together.
• Suggestions and criticisms offered and received in a helpful spirit.
• Co-operation not competition.
• High but not perfectionist standards.
• Good group-work expectations.
• Creativity stimulated.
• Ample communications.
• Discernment and decisiveness.
• Members challenged but not overburdened.

- Recognised, suitable leadership.
- Regular repentance – personal and corporate (2 Chron.7:14).
- Regular prayer, laughter and tears together (develop empathy).
- Regular learning together (develop humility).
- Regular review of progress (monitoring and evaluation).

Change Management

Change is inevitable. It is one of life's certainties! It may be enforced or chosen. In this e-generation, the rate of doubling of information is now approaching one year only, whereas in 1900 it had taken 100 years for global knowledge (data) to double. There may be an opportunity to be proactive about desirable change. The huge rate of knowledge accumulation possible and inflicted in the computer age needs a parallel application of timeless wisdom. We need to be able to sift wheat from an abundance of chaff! All change is dynamic, and involves both action and reaction. It always involves adjustments, some of these uncomfortable. Most people are naturally conservative and secure in the familiar, thus resistant to change. However, change means leaving the familiar for the unknown, as Abraham famously did (Gen.12:1; Heb.11:8-10). Many church people ask "how can we attract new members?" followed by "but we don't want any changes round here!." Actually, Christian conversion means radical change within and without.

Change management involves changing people (hopefully with courtesy) as well as changing circumstances. It involves creating innovative change as well as responding to imposed change. It has been said in dynamic organisations, "if you can't change the people's approach, change the people!" Good change management facilitates understanding of purpose, procedures and people. It is important to understand people's fears in the context of change. For instance, will they be able to cope, will they lose status, will they have to acquire new skills, will they need to work harder/longer? Changes that promise to improve effectiveness might be first tested experimentally rather than introduced as instant permanent replacements for the existing practices.

People can be grouped according to their change response. In relation to new ideas, technologies, opportunities, there are innovators, then early adopters, next the early majority, then the late majority and finally the laggards (reluctant; maybe suspicious; maybe lazy…). Christians should change in response to a "holy dissatisfaction" with things as they are. That's how pioneers think and how reformers envision and implement. *"Only dead fish move with the tide"* describes the pioneering spirit of enterprise, ambition, courage and adventure.

People will be motivated to change if they understand and approve of the purpose and targets towards which the change is directed. This is more likely if they have participated in setting those targets and the indicators by which they can judge for themselves whether or not they are attaining them. Development practitioners and church leaders are change agents whose influence can positively (or negatively) impact innovativeness (or fatalism).

Pitfalls of change include low morale owing to previous disappointment with change, especially if it was "change for change's sake" as with some bureaucracies and political regimes. Sometimes changes are attempted too much and/or too soon.

It is the role of leaders and Boards of Organisations to facilitate change. This means:-

a.   helping organisations to adapt to imposed change;
b.   anticipating changes "on the horizon;"
c.   instigating change to improve communication, effectiveness, resource stewardship;

d. welcoming and seeking constructive suggestions for change from team and outsiders;

e. Praying about change – especially conversion and discipleship development.

What Is Good Governance?

The Bible points clearly to the framework for good public governance – *Blessed is the nation whose God is the LORD* (Psalm 33:12); *Righteousnessexalts a nation but sin is a reproach to any people* (Proverbs 14:34);

> *God ... made from one [common origin, one source, one blood] all nations of people to settle on the face of the earth, having definitely determined [their] allotted periods of time and the fixed boundaries of their habitation - their settlements, lands and abodes; so that they should seek God, in the hope that they might feel after Him and find Him, although He is not far from each one of us.*
> — Acts 17:26,27 - *Amplified* Bible

There is now a global civil society. There can be no governance without consent, and the Bible clearly indicates proper government in the church with its instructions for the recognition of elders and the appointment of evangelists, pastors and teachers to enable all members to engage in integral mission (Eph.4:12). It does not prescribe church hierarchies! Nationally, good governance is a matter of opinion as to its details but, broadly, it provides a proper framework of behaviour for individuals in family, church, community and nation within international civil society.

At national level, "good" governments should be characterised by:

• Emphasis on their primary task of setting/maintaining **law and order** simply and equitably (this includes **protocols** for orderly movement of traffic and of market goods)

• Separate **legislature**

- Separate criminal and civil justice systems
- Ensuring **necessary services** are available for civil society, especially its weaker citizens [NB Services need not all be provided by government but may be provided by voluntary agencies and the private sector e.g. refuse collection and recycling, telephones...]
- **Defending** the nation's boundaries and heritage against external and internal attack
- **Minimising bureaucracy** and petty restrictions to business activity, civil liberty, Press freedom
- **Vision** concerning long term issues such as climate change, GMOs (Genetically-modified organisms), Food Chain matters, Water ...

An ancient Chinese proverb says:

> If there is righteousness in the heart,
> there will be beauty in the character;
> If there is beauty in the character,
> there will be harmony in the home;
> If there is harmony in the home,
> there will be order in the nation;
> When there is order in each nation,
> there will be peace in the world.

This approach chimes well with the Bible which identifies the human heart as needing to be changed in order to transform society. *Above all else, guard your heart, for everything you do flows from it.* (Prov.4:23). Ezekiel 36:26 offers "a new heart" as God's cure for sin. Jesus identified the "heart" as the source of all behaviour; *from inside proceed outward actions* (Matt.12:34-35). Many seem to believe that if one changes the political system, it will work, but the Bible says that the heart is deceitful above all things (Jer.17:9); change needs to start there.

Many issues are now clearly international and must be addressed on a global scale – including earth-care, climate change, defence, managing the movement of people, goods and services across boundaries, ocean fishing, and trading policy – especially in farm produce. International global protocols are needed to establish governance to manage these matters much more wisely. The Micah Network is concerned to see justice done in these ways (visit https:// www.micahchallenge.org/).

Romans chapter 13 offers advice in relation to submission to the authorities of government, behaving properly towards others, paying due taxes so that the weak may be helped but the Bible also records the arrest and questioning of Jesus (John 18:12-14; 19-24) and his subsequent false trial before Pilate, the Roman Governor (John 18: 28-40; John 19:1-16). What do these passages teach us about how to behave towards the cause of good governance by complying with legitimate requirements and resisting unjust issues? Where does the heart come into it?

> Let's pray for our own governments
> and play our part as directed by the Lord Jesus Christ
> in our own families, churches, communities,
> nations and internationally.

Board Development Criteria

In their own operation, boards need to reflect the principles underlying the organisation they serve, thus contributing positively to its ethos. Helping to set up accountable boards is a key part of integral mission training.

Definition of a Board

- Group of trustees / governors / directors / council members / elders
- In addition to a board, many organisations operate a separate *Reference Panel or Advisory Council* which usually has no legal status

in relation to the organisation but acts as a "check and balance" on the board, as a fund of wisdom or, owing to the reputation of its members, may add the credibility of proven experience to the organisation.

Roles of the Board:

Support, represent, pray, discern, challenge, inspire, care, love

- Oversight, vision, responsibility, stewardship, trusteeship, guidance, leadership
- NOT usurping management, nor the role of the management committee if there is one
- The board is legally responsible for the fulfilment of the aims and objectives of the organisation as set out in its **constitution** through the executive staff to whom responsibility is delegated to implement these on a day-to-day basis. Thus, the board has oversight and pastoral care duties towards these staff (or partners in the venture). In addition, board members may be expected to advocate on behalf of the organisation (in terms of promotion for funding, for potential users of its services or, if necessary, in its legitimate defence). Its members may offer technical as well as pastoral expertise to support its executive team.

Board Constitution

- Legal document describing composition, powers/limits, duties, *quorum*, meeting intervals
- The constitution should strike a balance between flexibility and clarity of terms of reference for the proper running of the organisation.

Composition and Life Cycle

* Membership, representation, length of service, re-election in rotation (not all at once!)
* A balance should be sought of male and female members, older/experienced and younger/new-blood members, local and more distant/outsider members. Between them, the members of the board should represent the range of relevant skills and experience needed within the terms of reference of the organisation.

Conduct and Leadership Style

* Openness, non-hierarchy, informality, humour, challenge of *status quo*; firm but relaxed.
* Suitably balanced concern for task achievement with maintenance of relationships. Jesus has been described as the 200% Person - i.e. 100% orientated towards task achievement and 100% orientated to personal relationship maintenance in the process (see Linkenfelter and Mayers, 1986). Overall, team spirit should be sought and maintained (Eph.4:3).

Contact with Practice

* Board members need awareness, field experience and regular subsequent exposure (so that they can act as friendly but objective "outsiders")
* In addition, it can be helpful to have members who are non-specialists in the area of work for which the organisation is set up in order that they bring a fresh objectivity to issues - using their "sanctified common sense" rather than risking over-reliance on specialist technical knowledge above reliance on the Spirit of God!

Co-operation

• Teamwork is the essence; balance of represented skills and experience; mutual respect.
• The board should also be constantly on the look-out for new people and ideas relevant to the healthy development of the organisation and its networking opportunities.

Competences

• Continuing Professional Development CPD or LLL (Lifelong Learning) are vital for all.
• CPD (LLL) is necessary not only for paid staff but also for Board members. When staff workshops are arranged, it is a good idea also to invite board members to attend some sessions and interact with the staff team.
• The board needs to understand the dynamics of change management and its members may need to acquire skills and "tools" for this process.

Conferencing

• Consultations, collaboration, networking; use telephone/ Skype/ Zoom "virtual" meetings.
• The board, if outward-looking and forward-thinking, will plan to hold "brainstorming" days with other relevant people and organisations in order to further the cause for which their organisation exists.

A board has a ruling role, equivalent to the "Masters" of Colossians 3:1- 4:6. Such masters are seen in scripture as "under-shepherds" i.e.

operating under Christ, the Chief Shepherd (1 Peter 5:1-4). Servant leadership is envisaged so that the organogram would look like a series of concentric circles (or the layers of an onion) with the cross central, "beneficiaries" around that, followed by paid staff and partner organisations next and board members and trustees in the outer circle where they can look out for external factors related to the legal and constitutional operation of the organisation and inwards to take seriously their governance responsibilities having regard to their pastoral and oversight role towards staff and those served.

Guidelines for Chairing Effective Meetings[1]

* **Be friendly** - start by trying to establish goodwill.
* **Be realistic** - don't try to achieve too much at first.
* **Be attentive** - listen really well; don't interrupt.
* **Be inquisitive** - check and show understanding – you mean??
* **Be honest** - say what you think and feel.
* **Be flexible** - admit your mistakes.
* **Be tolerant** - do not try to adjust their behaviour too much.

Role-play Exercises for Boards:

A. "Imagine you are the board of a relief organisation seeking to appoint staff to address conflict resolution in your region, holding its first meeting and assigning board tasks and preparing to recruit personnel."

B. "Imagine you are the founder members of a new board for an integral mission organisation being started to seek to reach those 'hard to reach.' Draft your constitution and agree the vision

---

[1]Based on notes from Peter Renwick FIDP

statement, mission statement and consequently required Board composition."

Your Observations and Questions

- A time for comment, debate and conclusions will be held with a view to:
- Producing a set of **ACTION POINTS** for the improvement of operation of the board, its executive committee(s), its trustees and its advisory council/reference panel.

Strategic Planning

Planning is "using time now to save time later." A prerequisite of planning is prayer, with due consideration of whose objectives? Whose expectations? Whose genuine wishes and needs? Tools used in seeking answers to these questions include: social mapping; natural esource mapping; stakeholder analysis through a local development forum. Collating the mass of information gleaned during strategic planning is assisted by the use of the Logical Framework Analysis tool (see below).

The Strategic Planning sequence involves:

1. **Information/needs assessment** (social and natural resource mapping etc.).
2. **Values** (agreed to underpin the approach of the organisation or community concerned).
3. **Vision** (stated hopes/aspirations - encapsulated in a phrase).
4. **Mission** (the service aims - what will be done encapsulated in brief strapline).
5. **Organisational assessment** (estimation of capacity to deliver its aims).
6. **Goal-Setting** (what and by when?).
7. **S.W.O.T.** (Strengths, Weaknesses, Opportunities, Threats) Analysis of present position.
8. **Choice of strategies** (which is to be selected to seek to achieve the goals set?).
9. **Objectives formulated** (SMART = specific measurable attainable realistic timed).
10. **Programmes? Projects?** (which ones are going already, which are envisaged?).
11. **Management** (personnel and resource allocation?).
12. **Organisational structure** (who is doing what; effect on existing work?).
13. **Action plan:** activity/time/persons/ resources/targets/ indicators/cost per objective.
14. **Risk assessment:** anticipation of what could happen, its probability and mitigation.

15. **Budget** - per Programme and per Project.
16. **Monitoring and evaluation:** indicators? frequency? by whom? Reports to?

Logical Framework Analysis ("Logframes")

This a planning and monitoring tool producing a one-page summary:

	Summary	OVI*	MOV**	Assumptions
Goal				
Purpose				
Outputs				
Activities				

* OVI = Objective Verifiable Indicators;
** MOV = Means of Verification

Questions regarding Hierarchy of Objectives

1. Where do we want to be? = **goal, purpose.**
2. How will we achieve these? (Project delivery methods) = **outputs, activities.**
3. How will we know we got there? = **indicators.**
4. What will show we got there? = **evidence.**
5. What problems *en route* might be expected? = **risks and assumptions.**

Why Logframe?

• Helps people get thinking logically and in an organised way.
• Helps identify weaknesses in project design.

- Ensures key indicators are identified.
- Ensures all those involved in the project use the same terminology and "own" it.
- Helps people to summarise a project plan.

Limitations of the Logframe

- It can make project management rigid/inflexible.
- Needs good leadership and facilitation skills to work well.
- Not appropriate in closed cultures.
- Terminology could be threatening.
- Interpretation can be difficult.
- Can exclude those already marginalised owing to its rather academic approach.
- Can ignore less easily measured factors such as ethos, community spirit, morale.
- Must involve both primary and secondary stakeholders.

Hierarchy of Objectives in the Logframe

- These relate to the objectives derived from an "objective tree" analysis.
- **GOAL** = to solve the main problem that gave rise to the project proposal.
- This goal should be stated in terms of "having achieved it" e.g. "improved health results."
- Only *one* purpose should be covered per logframe and thus done thoroughly.

Risk Analysis

- Look at the objectives of the project;

- If proposed activities are done, what can stop the intended outputs being achieved?
- If proposed outputs are achieved, what can stop the GOAL itself being achieved?
- An Impact Probability Matrix can be used to document this risk analysis:

	Impact →	Low	Medium	High
Probability	Low			
Probability	Medium			
Probability	High			

After listing risks 1,2,3 etc on the Logframe, one can then turn the risk statement into a positive assumption e.g. "rains reliable" having *estimated* the probability of them not being reliable! In this way, "if so, then what" test can be done across the logframe.

Project Management, Monitoring & Evaluation

A project is a planned period of activity towards a particular God-given goal or goals.

A project may involve government, co-ordinating authorities (maybe NGO), project manager, sub-managers, field workers and project users (beneficiaries).

Project sequence

1. **Pre-requisites** for **Project Managers:**
    - clear idea of what is to be done in partnership with all users (not just "target" population).

- establish co-ownership with project participants.
- be able to state constraints and directives governing the project.
- establish manageable units within the overall project.
- prepare a written schedule (timetable) for the project.
- seek understanding of perspectives of all people whose work affects the project.
- develop excitement and commitment of a team.
- listen to others more than talking yourself.
- build effective agreements through your negotiating skills.
- take time to nurture willing followers of your lead.
- stimulate the imagination (vision) and creativity among all people involved.
- be flexible to revise your approach realistically as need arises.
- show patience, remembering that "slow and sure" beats "flashy and failing."

2. **Preparatory survey** – of realities "on the ground" (sites, resources, constraints).

3. **Project plan** – based on feasibility studies, an agreed amended draft, with dates.

4. **Project design details** – ensuring technical suitability and practicality.

5. **Project implementation** – with benchmarked standards and timetabled.

6. **Project progress reporting** – concise, systematic, against established indicators.

7. **Project evaluation** – how far have project results met its own values and targets?

8. **Project replication** – if it was a pilot scheme, but with suitable local adaptation.

9. **Project scale and support services** – budget carefully with replicated projects .

10. **Avoid "Projectitis"** – whereby progress is deemed impossible without 'projects.'

11. **A project** should always be the simplest solution…avoid wasting leaders' time.

12. **Negotiating skills for project managers:** self-confidence; intelligence (to marshal and analyse information); conceptualisation; goal-setting; relationship-building (establishing mutual trust); asking open questions (What do you think? How might we tackle this?…); listening (first to God, then to others…).

Disaster Management

Disasters are of four principal kinds but vary as to scale of territory or population affected:

A. Sudden natural – as in earthquakes, tsunamis, hurricanes, floods.

B. Insidious natural – as with creeping soil erosion, drought-induced famines.

C. Chronic political – e.g. accumulation of IDPs (internally displaced persons) and refugees.

D. War-related – thus addressed by monitoring the news, political realities, sudden raids.

The Bible refers frequently to disasters and calamities – often the direct consequence of defying God (Deut.32:35) but also the result of living in a fallen world (Psa.18:18). It also advises preparedness as part of good discipleship (Luke 14:27-31) and taking refuge in God during disasters (Psa.57:1). The Bible warns against rejecting wisdom (Prov.1:20-31).

For instance, if people greedily build houses on flood plains then there should be no surprise when flood damage occurs. Furthermore, corrupt behaviour reaps its own disastrous rewards (Prov.6:12-15). However, those who gloat over the calamities overtaking the poor will not go unpunished (Prov.17:5). Instead, compassion compels a response to their plight. The poorest tend to suffer most in disasters and from the subsequent effects of them. Gloating over enemies who are overtaken by disasters is likewise condemned (Prov.24:17-22). Disaster is often equated with punishment and judgement in the OT (e.g. Jer.46:21). However, there is mercy for widows and orphans (Jer.49:7-11) and disaster situations are not to be exploited for gain (Obadiah 13). Jesus warned that the earth's future involves disaster before God's kingdom is established on it (Matt.24) and Paul warned the Thessalonians (1 Thess.5:3-4) to be alert, not expecting perpetual peace and safety on earth. Yet there are many who espouse the folly that tomorrow will be as today but much more prosperous (Isa.56:12). Many accept theories based on uniformitarianism i.e. that assume constant conditions on earth over millennia – despite abundant evidence to the contrary of catastrophism (including of the Genesis Flood, together with contemporary tsunamis, extreme weather events, earthquakes, and planning by astro-scientists to seek to avert cosmic impacts). The Christian faith involves trusting God in an uncertain present world. That trust includes using wise strategies to prepare for disasters and to manage risks. There is a place for God-appointed watchmen (Ezek.33:7).

With this Biblical background, disaster management includes:

1.   Warnings – including Biblical teaching on wise practices, reconciliation, peace-building.
2.   Risk assessments, mitigation strategies, and due preparation for disaster prevention.

3.   Search, rescue, relief, rehabilitation, reconstruction, re-establishment of civil society.
4.   Networking on it with Government, NGOs, Red Cross, community leaders and locals.
5.   Planning the logistics of responses in supplying basic water, food and shelter to victims.
6.   Specialist services such as evacuation procedures, identifying/protecting stray children.
7.   Monitoring the situation on warehousing of goods, including medicines/public health.

Those engaged in disaster management must not usurp the initiatives of local people. Wise local leaders will know who is genuinely needy in their communities. They will also be likely to have detailed local knowledge of resources and realities – although they may be overwhelmed by the scale of a disaster that is already familiar to a disaster management professional from elsewhere. Local survivors must be recruited into the efforts of recovery and rehabilitation. This may well prove every bit as effective as professional trauma counselling in their own coming to terms with the harsh situation that has arisen, although such Christian counselling also has its key role in disaster responses. Learning from the history of past disasters is wise. Resilience needs to be conserved within natural resource management, such as adopting systems of farming that supply local food using local resources such as composts and natural pesticides, capture of roof water and sustainable fuelwood cultivation and use through fuel-efficient stoves. Communities with strong civil societies at peace within are more able to withstand and respond to disasters than those in conflict beforehand. *Be Prepared* is the motto of the International Scout Movement. Disciples should prepare for disasters too!

Chapter 8

Social Aspects

Civil Society and Social Action in Development

Civics concerns the rights and responsibilities of citizenship for all citizens everywhere. However, "rights" language can be very emotive and this writer prefers as the Christian counter-balance to stress "responsibilities," and the concept of "God-favoured common grace." Nevertheless, social action and even civil disobedience may sometimes be legitimate in the pursuit of what God desires via his common grace. Scripture frequently records, recognises and endorses teamwork and social mobilisation to achieve God's purposes - a cord of three is not easily broken (Eccl.4:12). Exodus 20:1-17 contains the 10 commandments indicating God's standards for societal harmony. The twelve disciples achieved huge social impact. We should pray for those in authority (Romans 13).

Evangelism or Social action?

The so-called social gospel of the late 19th and early 20th centuries became associated with a liberal approach to theology and thus became falsely set against the camp of those who stressed evangelism and a conservative view of Biblical truth. Actually, evangelism and social responsibility go together. A wholistic theology is one which faithfully seeks to reflect Biblical reality where 'word and deed' combine in integral mission. Jesus modelled how to intervene; Jesus was wholistic, redemptive, radically inclusive and institution-wary (Stephens, 1998). He dared to engage, and especially engaged, in non-religious contexts.

Social dimensions of international development

Social service (provision of relief, welfare and development services) should be distinguished from social action (social ministry geared towards changing social structures). However, participatory approaches to development training may enable delivery of both social services and social action. Understanding of cultures must precede gospel-inspired social transformation efforts. Social action involves teamwork and an extension of that to include mobilisation of whole societies. The motivation for social action arises from at least two categories; firstly, positive mutuality on the basis that "two heads + hands + hearts are better than one" in executing a useful work, and secondly that many cases of social injustice exist worldwide and require countervailing collective power. (W)holistic empowerment is the outcome of a Biblical ethic for development (Ajulu, 2001). Many examples can be cited including the collapse of communism and apartheid. Globalisation has highlighted some of these injustices as worldwide phenomena affecting environment and society and demanding restorative justice pursued through social action. A current need for focus is World Trade Organisation (WTO) policy change, particularly as it impacts food supplies and natural resource management. There is the vital ongoing concept of intergenerational justice as we consider earth's finite environment (see Environment section).

Civil Society and Public Theology

Venter (2004) reports *Doing Reconciliation,* notably in South Africa, and argues the case for a **human rights focus** in the fight against racism and violence in society (with echoes of the famous 1960s speeches of Dr Martin Luther King). There is such a thing as **"public theology."** Acting together, each person can make a difference towards a better world. The Bible recognises the validity of claims by genuinely underprivileged minorities (such as "the poor"). It also recognises the spiritual battle between prevailing cultural concepts and the kingdom of God with its Living Lord - with Paul's proviso *If it is possible, as far as it depends on you, live at peace with everyone* (Rom.12:18). By active engagement, one can influence policy formulation, join with others in solidarity campaigning for a cause in line with Biblical ethical principles even though not all those so campaigning share a Biblical perspective. In such ways, it is possible to multiply influence far beyond what one may imagine since *all things are possible with God* (Mark 10:27). This is **public discipleship** which is God pleasing as well as forming the basis for good governance.

There is a positive Biblical mandate for social action. The late Dr John Stott considered it is not a case of *either* evangelism *or* social action but *both/and* in the Bible's holistic theology, supported especially by accounts of the ministry of Jesus, thus mandating integral mission.

Civil society needs to harness the collective common sense of the majority of most populations, with Christians engaged and infused as disciples representing the "salt and light" of the gospel (Matt.5:13-16). To do this, Christians need to serve within the institutions of civil society. Such calling should be encouraged by wise church leaders even though it may preclude a person's greater availability to serve in specifically church-related organisations.

Social action in a responsible way is necessary for three main reasons:

1. It strengthens communal relationships by mutual work towards common concerns;
2. Task achievement is potentially more effective and efficient through co-ordinated collaboration (viz. Nehemiah e.g. Neh.4:6,16-18);
3. Oppression from dictators, bad lawmakers and bureaucracies requires the countervailing power of public solidarity to combat it.

Micah Network, started by *Tearfund* Australia pursues justice: https://www.micahchallenge.org.

Advocacy

Advocacy means "to speak for and with others" – to be "a voice for the voiceless," to intercede, to support or defend a cause, "to plead on behalf of" as in a court of law, as far as possible involving the stakeholders. Advocacy might be on behalf of God, of other people or of the rest of creation. "Advocate" in scripture is translated "Comforter" (*Parakletos* = "one alongside to help") as of the Lord Jesus (1 John 2:1) or the Holy Spirit (John 14:16).

Amazingly, God has chosen to use us as his mouthpieces not only in preaching, teaching and prophesying (telling forth his messages) but also in simply "gossiping the gospel" in our daily lives. As such, he has largely chosen to be voiceless until we speak for him. "Christ has no hands but ours" as goes St Teresa of Avila's prayer. This places a huge responsibility upon us to *correctly handle the word of truth* (2 Tim 2:15) by discerning what the will and purposes of God are through understanding, appreciation and application of Biblical truths by the inspiration of the Holy Spirit. The church's mission is to set forth and to defend the whole counsel of God, as summed up in the Ten Commandments - not just ten suggestions, as somebody once said! (Exodus 20:1-17; see also 2 Tim.3:16).

Then we are to speak up for other people to those who have power to respond helpfully to their needs, notably policy-makers and politicians. We are to speak for those unable to speak for themselves owing to being too young, too old, too infirm, too inarticulate, too oppressed, tradition-bound, deliberately marginalised or disabled (Proverbs 31:8-9). Though we wish to adopt a wider definition, it is usually taken that advocacy refers specifically to this important activity on behalf of other people, often to combat and seek equity to rectify social injustice. Issues involved may include:- life itself (including anti-abortion, pro-life advocacy), gender-based deprivation (such as lack of education for the girl-child), minority ethnic groups, HIV/AIDS, freedom of movement, freedom of speech, freedom of religion, access to basic needs of water, food, shelter, clothing, warmth, creative work, adequate rest, transparent voting systems, fair trials, legal representation, racial non-discrimination, education and training, special needs provision and poverty alleviation in general. Community, societal, national and international levels are included, especially in reconciliation and conflict resolution work. Those who are able should exercise their responsibilities and seek equity.

Finally, the rest of creation "groans in pain together" as Paul put it (Romans 8:22). We are to speak up for God's indicated standards of welfare and stewardship with concerned companionship and in the priestly role for creation which he has delegated to us (Psalm 115:16; Psalm 150:6). It is particularly in the areas of environmental ethics and animal welfare that voice can be given on behalf of creation. This would include responsible action to combat global warming, desertification, land degradation, unjust trading, pollution and wasteful use of energy. It would include promotion of conservation of soil, water, landscapes, sustainable livelihoods worldwide for those 'there to care' as farmers, land and sea-users.

In short, advocacy is about getting involved and being part of the answer to our Lord's taught prayer *Thy Kingdom come, Thy will be done on earth as it is in heaven* (Matthew 6:10), about *seeking first the Kingdom of God* (Matthew 6:33), about urging and working for Kingdom values until he (Jesus) returns. It requires a firm but prayerful approach to those in power (e.g. Nehemiah 2:5 *Then I prayed to the God of heaven, and I answered the king,* and Romans 13). We need the Holy Spirit within and ever before us in the task of advocacy.

"Human Rights" or Responsibility to Pursue Justice.

The Bible has much to say about justice and about responsibilities in relation to it, including advocating for it. The psalmist (Psa.99:4,5) reminds us that *The King is mighty, he loves justice – you have established equity; in Jacob you have done what is just and right.* Abraham did not claim "rights" but rather trusted God to "do right" (Gen.18:25). William Wilberforce et al over 200 years ago campaigned against slavery on the basis of right (justice) not "rights." Jesus taught responsible resource use within our limitations (Matt.25:14ff.). It is recognised that many of those using the term "Human rights" in a secular context are well-intentioned to protect the weak; nevertheless, the term needs critical examination from a Biblical standpoint. A "Rights" mindset implies "I deserve" and shouts "give me" thus creating dependency, stifling the "can do" mentality which is the basis of dignity, self-esteem and wholistic development. A "responsibility" mindset, on the other hand, says *let me look out for the needy* (Phil.2:4) – whether needy for help through infancy, old age, infirmity or other, sometimes temporary, weakness. "Justice" calls for those capable to exercise responsibility, which is an active behaviour effective when driven by compassion (love in action, central to the Christian response). The Bible is full of examples calling us to emulate God in whose image we are created, such as the psalmist's call (Psa.68:5) to care for the fatherless and widows. Isaiah (58:5-14) contrasts the sighing "poor me" culture with the kind of service he is seeking. "Rights" language leads us into a passive "poor me" or "poor them" culture, instead of taking up the call to the able and strong to act responsibly, including bringing about systemic justice throughout society. That involves being a "voice for the voiceless" and "advocate for the weak" NOT on the basis that they have "rights" but rather that God's justice demands that the stronger serve those in need.

In secular usage, it is taken as self-evidently correct and indisputable that everyone has "the right to life, to liberty, to fresh air, water, self-actualisation etc." However, these are gifts of God by grace, not rights of humans. The Bible talks of "birth right," for example in the case of Esau who "sold his birth right for a bowl of food" when hungry. However, the context makes it clear that he was irresponsible in doing so and the term "birth right" was an expression of the established system whereby children had a "family-designated inheritance." Now, of course, not all systems of inheritance are equitable, or just. Indeed, the Bible is full of examples of injustice and there are plenty of cases today. These are causes for redoubling efforts to establish justice and taking **responsibility** to do so; they do not require the concomitant application of "rights" language. It is here argued that "rights" language confuses the issue when it is those suffering injustice who need a voice for them plus action to correct their plight. Responsible behaviour seeking justice will deliver the kingdom values that will be right for all.

In working towards this now by living Kingdom values, the prophet Micah 6:8 asserts that the duty of humans is to *To act justly and to love mercy and to walk humbly with your God;* no mention of "rights"! The Bible's analysis of the human condition is that

> *all have sinned and fall short of the glory of God, and all are justified*
> *freely by his grace through the redemption that came by Christ Jesus.*
> —Romans 3:23,24

It is 100% grace; there is no room for "rights" (Eph.2:8; Phil.2:1-11). We deserve nothing but the wrath of God and only grace mediated through the cross of Christ can save us. It was "amazing grace" not "rights" that saved slave-trader John Newton. We are challenged to become servant helpers of any who are less able to provide for themselves than we may be, by God's grace at a particular time. We are to advocate for justice and for responsibility via integral mission.

Justice is a societal concept whereby we seek mutual sharing, equity and inter-relationships of caring. *Do unto others as you would have them do unto you* is a common moral value of many societies as well as a scriptural principle – but the Bible goes further, as when Jesus challenges His followers to *But I tell you, love your enemies and pray for those who persecute you* (Matt. 5:44).

The sufferer in this instance is not incited to cry for "rights" but rather to meet injustices with love. The grace of God in the life of President Nelson Mandela showed the world the triumph of responsibility and justice over cries for revenge and "rights." "Rights" language is confrontational, while "Responsibility" language is conciliatory as the behaviour is directed towards justice, peace and the integrity of creation.

Peace-Building Through Conflict Resolution & Reconciliation

Peace

The Biblical prescription for peace lies in Jesus Christ, whose blood shed on the cross brings us to God (Eph. 2:12-22). Wise use of the tongue helps to preserve peace while its misuse threatens peace (James 3). Processes of demilitarisation will herald God's Kingdom (Zech.9:10) as promised by Isaiah 32:13-20 – notably verse 14, *The fruit of that righteousness will be peace; its effect will be quietness and confidence for ever.* Jesus promised His peace to the disciples (John 14:27) having earlier pronounced peacemakers to be blessed sons of God (Matt.5:9). Paul exhorts the church (Phil.4:1-9) to avoid disagreement promising that then *the peace of God, which transcends all understanding, will guard your hearts and minds in Christ Jesus ... and the God of peace will be with you* (vv.7 and 9).

Conflict Resolution

This requires recognition of the sources, sites and key solutions for conflict:

- **Sources of conflict:** greed, scarcity, lust, power, pride, status (Prov.6:16-19).
- **Sites of conflict** include: self (Jer. 17:9; Mark 7:20-23; Jas.4:1-5; Rom.7:18,19); family (Gen.37:28); community (Lev.19:13-18); nations (Psa.2:1-4)
- **Solutions for conflict** include: *In your anger do not sin: do not let the sun go down while you are still angry* (Eph.4:26); name, admit shame and repent of sins (admit, back down, confess, talk through – "jaw, jaw beats war, war" said British Prime Minister Winston Churchill.

There must be genuine humble prayer and repentance, then God will not only forgive sins but heal the land (2 Chron.7:14). There must be a desire for that forgiveness – and a willingness to receive it and to give it to others who have hurt us, coupled with endeavour to forget those hurts. God's gift of forgiveness is signified by giving the believer a new heart (Ezek.36:26). Such believers then submit to God and to each other (Jas. 4:6-12). They endeavour to maintain the unity of the spirit (Eph.4:3) and live according to Romans 8. The result will be *shalom,* God's all-conquering peace (Isa.2:2-4) leading to reconciliation.

Reconciliation

Greek *katallage* means "exchange" (while *apokatallasso* means "complete transformation"). Reconciliation thus leads to "restored relationships" – to God, within oneself, towards neighbours, and towards the earth. It is interpersonal, intercommunal and springs especially from awareness of one's own sin. It follows only from **truth, justice** and **forgiveness** (Christian imperatives in civil society). It links with the theology of Atonement through the blood of Jesus shed on the cross, providing justification by faith. It is enabled powerfully when we are deeply conscious of our own need for God's forgiveness. Full reconciliation is a sovereign work of God the Father, Son and Holy Spirit. Reconciliation needs VIM: Vision of what you want to become; **I**ntention to act; **M**eans to do it. It requires realistic, open sharing and exposure of what went wrong to spoil relationships. It is based upon the value of each soul and of restoring justice. Reconciliation is pursued by developing friendships, setting up groups, sharing mutual life-stories, Biblical teaching, services and acts of restitution, trips together, work together on mutually needed projects such as on community water supplies, litter removal, tree-planting... Indeed, RURCON advocates for reconciliation as a prerequisite for sustainable community development. Biblical cases cited by RURCON Friend Alexander Venter in South Africa include:

- Old Testament:- Gen.3-4; Gen.25-33; Gen.37, 42-45; Josh.22; 2 Sam 11-12, Psa.51; I Kings 21.
- New Testament gospel cases:- Matt.5:21-26;6:12;18:15-35; Lk.10:30-36; Lk.15:11-32; Lk.19:1-10; Jn.1:4-42;
- Other New Testament cases: Acts 6:1-7; 9:1-31; 10; Gal.2:11-16; Philemon; Gal.3:26-29; Eph.2:11-22; 2 Cor.5:16-21.

Migration

Migration has been a key part of the story of the children of Israel over their long history (e.g. Deut.8:2 *Remember how the LORD your God led you all the way in the wilderness*) and often owing to their disobedience (Psa.106). For centuries, they had no homeland and lived in diaspora worldwide until the establishment of the State of Israel in 1948. Many still live abroad. Migration is also part of the history and deliberate lifestyle of others, such as pastoralists in the Horn of Africa, the nomadic Fulani of West Africa, and the nomadic Maasai of East Africa. In the case of pastoralists, their travels are dictated by the seasonal availability of grazing for their livestock. They have adjusted their movements and lifestyles accordingly over hundreds of years. Climate change and changing pressures of population increase, both among and around them, have made their migrations more constrained in recent decades. Others have migrated regularly such as workers to the mines of RSA from neighbouring countries. However, a growing international concern is that of **enforced migration.** People flee from places of conflict, persecution and "ethnic cleansing" to safer zones, sometimes those artificially created by UN peace-keeping forces and other forms of sheltered accommodation. Others migrate owing to dire economic circumstances in the hope of finding jobs and livelihood opportunities elsewhere, often making hazardous journeys in their quest. Many migrants are internally-displaced persons (IDPs) within their home countries – such as some nations of the Middle East and Africa. It is reckoned in 2021 that there are some 272 million migrants globally i.e. 3.5% of world population. This raises a number of **aspects** for those seeking faithfully to pursue integral mission:

a. **Advocacy:** seeking to raise awareness and prompt solutions regarding causal factors;

b. **Direct ministry:** to those IDPs and international migrants in our operating areas;

c. **Training:** of church and community leaders to address migrant issues;

d. **Informing:** supporters and responsible governments on growing needs of migrants;

e. **Peace & reconciliation:** pursuing practical training and liaison to enable that.

RURCON has been involved in various ways, including among IDPs within Nigeria, and among Liberians from warring tribes found within the same refugee camp in Ghana.

It may be said that the ultimate sought outcome of integral mission is neatly summed up by the rural prophet Micah in his vision of the Mountain of the LORD in the last days:

> *Everyone will sit under their own vine and under their own fig-tree, and no-one will make them afraid, for the LORD Almighty has spoken.*

> —Micah 4:4

The burgeoning global migrant crisis is the antithesis of Micah's vision. Far too many people are suffering conflict and displacement through human greed and injustice. We are called to respond as co-workers with God seeking to minister His compassion for migrants, remembering the advice of Hebrews 13:2: *Do not forget to show hospitality to strangers, for by doing so some people have shown hospitality to angels without knowing it.*

Chapter 9

Case Studies

Jonah Commissioned

The Book of Jonah is historic occurring in the C8ᵗʰ BC, (2 Kings 14:25), and as affirmed by Jesus Christ in Matt.12:39-41 and Lk.11:29-32. Jonah, meaning "Dove" (peace-bringer) was a bigoted Jew, son of Amittai of Gath-hepher, in northern Israel (Josh.19:13). The Assyrian Empire collapsed in 765 BC (by mutual destruction of leaders, though repentance calls were often made, and it was revived in 745 BC); Nineveh (near Mosul in Iraq) was destroyed later (612 BC). It had a 60 miles perimeter wall with a top wide enough for chariots to pass.

The Book of Jonah is *not* a parable, neither is it just a fable, but history. There is universal knowledge of Jonah being swallowed. The King of Assyria (*& Melek Nineveh*) was Pul or, in full, *Tiglath-Pileser* III. This is known because *shah-puhi* or ritual repentance was demonstrated when he temporarily left his throne & wore sackcloth. Jonah's Mission to **Nineveh** was to preach repentance. There is conjecture about the nature of the monster that swallowed Jonah after he was tipped into the sea at his own request after running away from the task God had assigned to him. Some say it might have been a whale such as a *Cachalot* type of sperm whale up to some 20m long in the Mediterranean Sea, with a buccal cavity with dimensions of 4m

+ x 2m+ x 4m (metres). At least 3 men survived such swallowing in C20th. A lobster fisherman off Canada was swallowed in June 2021 and regurgitated by the whale from the darkness of its belly. However, one "monster" exhibited in Rome by Pliny the Elder alongside a "Ship of Tarshish" (oar-powered: *tarsos* = oar) was a *Ketos* or Dog-headed Sea Dragon. Chapter 1:

- vv. 1-2 **Commissioned:** arise, go, cry to that great city of Nineveh;
- v.3 **Disobedience:** flight, fall (went down), to find ship, fare (paid for it himself)
- v.4 **But God:** sent wind, storm (cf Matt.8:23-27; Mk.4:36-41; Lk. 8:22-25)
- vv. 5-16 **Jonah witnessing despite himself;** men tried to spare him at 1st
- v.17 **"Whale"** provided by God for 3 days & 3 nights … cf. Jesus in the tomb…

Key Lessons from Jonah:

- Creation, salvation & commission for service are inseparable
- God prefers to show mercy over judgement wherever possible
- Former Air Vice-Marshal in Saddam Hussain's Iraqi Cabinet Georges Sada dated the turning of his family to the God of the Bible at the time of Jonah's preaching. Jonah eventually sowed the seed
- Jesus acknowledged the historical Jonah and applied lessons from his real experience (Matt.12:39-42; Lk.11:29-32).

Proverbs Overview of Integral Mission Wisdom

Chapter themes and integral mission issues in the Book of Proverbs are instructive:

- 1: 1-7 Beginning of knowledge; 8-19 avoid evil advice; 20-33 heed Wisdom's call.
- 2: The value of Wisdom
- 3: Guidance
- 4: Security
- 5: Peril of adultery
- 6: 1-5 Dangerous promises; 6-11 folly of indolence; 12-19 the wicked person
- 6:20 – 7:5 Beware adultery; 7:6-27 a crafty prostitute
- 8: Excellence of Wisdom (and its personification in Christ vv.22-31)
- 9:1-12 The way of Wisdom; 13-18 the way of folly
- 10:1 – 22:16 The wise sayings of Solomon
- 22:17 – 24:34 Sayings of the wise (collation organised by Solomon)
- 25 – 29 Further wise sayings of Solomon
- 30 The wisdom of Agur
- 31:1-9 Words from King Lemuel's mother
- 31:10-31 The virtuous wife (an acrostic poem of parallel ideas).

Questions from Proverbs

a.   Where are the following and what do they indicate?:
       Ants; 2.herbs; 3.butter; 4.honey; 5.pig; 6.bear; 7.dog; 8.leech; 9.apple; 10.Ox.
b.   What are the following and in which verse(s) did you get your answer?
       Fear; 12.wrath antidotes; 13.in settings of silver; 14.medically sound hearts; 15.weeds indicative; 16.ways to get paths directed; 17.contents of house of the righteous.

Proverbs: Practical 'self' Issues

- Contrary voices – 1:10 but 9:10

- Treasure/submit to wisdom – 2:1,2; 22:17
- Paradox of riches – 14:11; 15:16
- Guidance – vital, relational, marital, healthy, economic – 3:5,6, 8,10; 4:11;15:6; 18:22; 19:14; 31:10-31
- Heart-care/Soul diligence– 4:23; 13:4; 15:13,15; 17:22; 27:19
- Seduction & HIV/AIDS – 5:11
- Receive correction – 3:12; 10:17; 15:5; 21:11;25:12
- *Counsellors of peace have joy* (12:20)
- *Envy rots the jealous* (14:30)
- *A soft answer turns away wrath* (15:1)
- *Pride goes before a fall* (16:18)

Practical Management Issues from Proverbs

- Committed works - thoughts 16:3
- Equitable trading – 11:1,26; 16:8,11; 20:10,23; 22:16
- Cultivations – 12:11; 20:4; 24:27; 24:30-34; 28:19
- Resource diligence – 12:27; 13:23; 14:4; 27:23
- Prompt discipline – 13:24; 19:18; 22:6,15; 23:13,14; 29:15,17
- Mandate to help poor/public theology 14:31,34
- Teamwork – 15:22; 24:6
- Nutrition – 16:24; 24:13; 25:16,27
- Strategic planning – 19:21; 20:18; 21:5,31; 27:1; 29:18
- Advocacy – 21:22; 31:8,9
- Good women in management/development 31:10-31

The Reckoning: pointers for moving on in IntegralMission

- Avoid gossip – 16:28; 18:8; 20:19; 26:20-22
- Self-control & calm spirit – 16:32; 17:27

- Questions? – 17:16; 20:6,9; 30:4; [2 Peter 3:9]
- True friendship -17:17; 18:24; 27: 6,7,17
- Beware 'one-man-bands' – 18:1
- Don't be too hale & hearty in early morning! 27:14
- Overlook transgressions – 19:11; 25:21,22
- Don't nag! – 19:3;21:9,19; 25:24; 27:15
- Avoid excess alcohol – 20:1; 23:20,21, 29-35

Key pointers for Integral Mission from Proverbs

- Seek refuge in God – 18:10
- Kindness> wealth/status – 19:22
- Beware! "riches make wings" – 23:4,5
- Observe landmarks/boundaries – 22:28; 23:10
- Fear God, not man – 29:25,26
- Pursue results don't get consequences! 30:33

Micah & Accountability

Micah's name asks a question and means *"Who is like Jehovah God?"* The Bible has several named Micah but the prophet was from Moresheth in Judah. Micah was a contemporary (c.750-700 BC) of the great prophet Isaiah, and prophesied during some 50 years in the reigns of Jotham, Ahaz and generally good king Hezekiah – whose conduit of clear water still leads into the old city of Jerusalem today (Jer.26:17-19). Micah was an ordinary countryman who prophesied the Messiah's birth in Bethlehem (5:2,7; Matt.2:5). He identified with the people in their sufferings (1:8). He writes plainly of sin, of judgement, of the despair people feel and yet of the hope in the gospel through integral mission. His summary of "true religion" in Micah 6:8 (Micah Network's key motto – https://www.micahnetwork.org) has been considered by many commentators over the centuries to be unsurpassed in its concise clarity. Micah has no time for *faith without works* nor for *works without faith* (James 2:17-18). He resists formalism in religion but applauds ethical outcomes from true faith. He poses questions but offers answers. He analyses present reality but has clear vision of God's agenda for His Kingdom. What a model for us to pursue! Where are we now?

Chapter 1 tells us that God abhors transgressions of idolatry and the temple sacrifices funded by prostitution (v.7). Verses 10-15 contain "plays" on Hebrew words: *Gath* = tell; *Acco* = weep; *Beth Ophrah* = house of dust; *Saphir* = pleasant; *Zaanan* = come out; *Beth Ezel* = standing nearby; *Maroth* = bitter; *Lachish* = team of draft animals; *Aczib* = deception; *Mareshah* = conqueror. God speaks in parables and in context.

Chapter 2 contrasts human and divine plans. It identifies the kind of preacher this dissolute people would like (v.11) yet promises deliverance for those who trust God with him as their Shepherd going ahead (v.13).

Chapter 3 rebukes leaders and prophets for "turning a blind eye" to injustices and pronounces judgement on negligence. Corruption leads to complacency, merits condemnation: "Zion will be ploughed as a field" (v.12).

Chapter 4 envisions God's plans for earth in the spheres of domestic order and of civil governance. It foretells the restoration of Kingdom values in practice. It is rich in rural metaphors. Conflict resolution and peace-building will lead to settled, sustainable and secure livelihoods for all (v.4). This is the exact opposite of what many in the world today experience with the growing numbers of homeless ones, of refugees and of migrants. The "farming tsunami" worldwide is currently forcing many out of their farms in an unregulated tidal flow of least-cost products. However, this great chapter begins with "But" applied to

God's plans and activity and ends with "consecration" of "substance" (material resources) *to the LORD of the whole earth* (v.13). Turning to God (vv.1-2a) leads to establishment of law (v.2b) which brings peace for food cultivation (v.3) and this means settled property – noting that this is livelihood-based property enjoyed by active people (v.4). The land belongs to God (Psa.24:1). We are only cast as tenants (Psa.115:16). Why can we be confident that people will be settled? – because *the mouth of the LORD of hosts has spoken it* (v.4b). Why can we be confident that people will be fed and sheltered? - because *the mouth of the LORD of hosts has spoken it* (v.4b). Why can we be sure of security, that "none shall make them afraid" - because *the mouth of the LORD of hosts has spoken it* (v.4b). More rural metaphors follow. Let us prepare with Kingdom work in Kingdom hope now!

Chapter 5 promises that Kingdom rule will centre on Jesus, the one born in Bethlehem (v.2) whose "greatness will reach to the ends of the earth" (v.4) and will Himself "be our peace" (v.5 and Eph.2:14). The Kingdom will involve deliverance from what is wrong and destruction of it, including idols (v.14) and disobedience (v.15).

Chapter 6 reminds us that the mountains and foundations of the earth stand witness to all that has taken place throughout history. No amount of ritual and sacrifices can compensate for that (vv.6,7). Only pure living will do (v.8). What a clear formula indeed of unambiguous guidance – *act justly and to love mercy and to walk humbly with your God;* these are the characteristics of the successful life, not accumulation of material wealth nor of power which characterised Israel's behaviour with ill-gotten gains and short measure (v.10) which merit judgement. Displacement through injustices – greed, conflict, war - displeases God.

Chapter 7 Israel's misery in her judged state is temporary because God will save to make her a people of promise because of who he is (v.18), and how he acts - true to his covenant (v.20). Forgiveness by God is the only hope for the future.

Practical Integral Mission Measures – A 30-Point Plan

1. More **FARMS** (Farm Asset Resource Management Study) Groups, locally-owned.
2. Model **primary schools** with farms using locally appropriate technologies can be crucial.
3. Academic, research and extension links with communities/schools.
4. Consider training/supporting *Key Farmer Trainers* for schools/communities.
5. Support short **field workshops** to catalyse improved existing **resource management.**
6. Support national construction of village **dams, springs & roof-water catchment tanks.**
7. Further encourage village/community shared **treadle pumps** for dry-season gardens.
8. Support extension of **appropriate-scale replicates** of successful farmers' ventures.
9. Support extension and supply of **"Starter Packs"** (seed etc) for beginner farmers.
10. Support, survey, research and develop **"conservation agriculture."**
11. Promote local processing (esp. **solar drying**) and improved household storage of foods.
12. Support the further development of money **"Switch"** cards for secure food trading.

13. Support development of mobile telephone masts for better food pricing "infonet."

14. Support **radio listening groups** in communities for sharing of practical experience.

15. Support subsidised (NOT free) tree/plant seedling/seed **banks** e.g. *Moringa, Artemisia.*

16. Advocate for each household **2-tree planting campaign** (1 fruit + 1 fodder/fuel-wood).

17. Dig shallower **pit-latrines** (but beware high water-tables) & subsequently plant banana.

18. Support **compost-making** training, including use of human urine

19. Support use of **natural pesticides,** & plants for medical/ veterinary uses (www.anamed.org).

20. Properly **house goats, pigs & poultry** (link to feed-rationing, better breeding, compost).

21. Encourage the use of **draft animals** for cultivations, power, and haulage of farm goods.

22. Promote improved, locally-made clay **fuel-efficient stoves** to at least double heat capture.

23. **Add value** to produce by drying or juicing fruits, making jam, cakes/biscuits, yoghurt.

24. Promote **household hygiene** with plate-drying racks and use of tip-taps plus soap.

25. Promote **bee-keeping** with improved hives and planting trees and other attractive crops

26. Promote "best kept" farm, household, village **competitions,** with polythene litter removal.

27. Encourage **"Junior Conservation Societies"** to form for environmental management.

28. Encourage **fish pond** construction to diversify diets and to save pressure on local lakes.
29. Encourage environmental monitoring and maintenance groups in communities.
30. Promote good resource management/info. via **church demonstration compounds.**

Action Points – as used at the end of all workshopson integral mission:

A. What points have you **learned** afresh or for the first time about practical actions?
B. With whom will you **share** these insights? With whom will you **network?**
C. What will you now **do** in the next 6 months with resources you control or influence?

Some Integral Mission Questions related to the Environment

1. Getting into **food** is getting off the track of preaching for eternity?
2. Some say, "My Bible tells me we are to get a new heaven and a **new earth** (Rev.21:1; 2 Peter 3:13): why bother so much about this earth. Trust God! …?"
3. Are **rights** right?
4. What is transformational development?
5. Why **care** for the environment?
6. What is the **New Age** movement? How does it relate to the "greening of mission?"
7. "Agriculture is central to the fight against poverty - physical and spiritual" - Discuss.

Creation Responsibility: Some Questions

1. Should we care, or is it beyond us?...
2. Do we care anthropocentrically – i.e. just to serve enlightened human self-interest?
3. For whom should we care? – as done for God and for his creation (human & non-human)?
4. Why should we care? – creation mandate/dominion covenant (Gen 1:26-28)...?
5. Where should we care? – land, sea and air – outer space?
6. When should we care? – lifelong, start early teaching responsibility & grace (not rights!)
7. How should we care? – as God's co-workers rather than panic-stricken environmentalists?

Obvious current issues include: Population and natural resources; climate change adaptation and mitigation; security of food + water + energy in a crowded, post peak-oil situation; rediscovering "enough" and *oikonomia*; the link between justice, peace & integrity of creation; the vital link between creation and salvation...

APPENDIX A. RESPONSES TO PRACTICAL TREE MANAGEMENT WORKSHOPS, 8 PLACES, MALAWI 2012

MCHIZANJALA ("Healing Hunger"): What have you learned/been reminded about? 18 attendees (60% male)	MCHIZANJALA: What will you do in next 6 months?
• Trees in the Bible (14) • Caring for trees (14) • Sustainability of life • Uses of trees (4) • Use of bamboo as water-pipe or gutter	• Teach how to plant & start a tree nursery • Start a tree nursery & sell seedlings (2) • Plant trees on eroded/erodible land • Expand conservation farming • Use tree guards • Build a fuel-saving stove • Help form FARMS Groups • Raise chickens & use their manure to make compost & "ring" trees against termites

KONGWE ("Cold"): What have you learned/been reminded about? 25 attendees (70% male) - 2 funerals	KONGWE: What will you do in next 6 months?
<ul><li>Why it is bad to destroy trees</li><li>Benefits and values of trees</li><li>Manure can also come from trees</li><li>Fuel-saving stoves</li><li>Importance of livestock care</li><li>Environment Care goes with spiritual life</li><li>Don't cultivate up to riverbanks</li><li>Raised livestock house can be home-made</li><li>Leucaena is animal feed (<25% ration)</li><li>Bees & trees benefit each other</li><li>Avoid cows & goats eating plastic</li></ul>	<ul><li>Plant trees : 10 – 25 each (12 people)</li><li>Plant 10 different kinds of tree</li><li>Establish a tree nursery (2)</li><li>Establish a conservation farming plot</li><li>Make a fuel-saving stove (5)</li><li>Teach how to make fuel saving stoves</li><li>Incorporate tree work in Farmers' Group</li></ul>
KASITU: What have you learned/been reminded about? 44 attendees (55% male, including 8 Chiefs) plus children & others	KASITU: What will you do in next 6 months?
<ul><li>Uses of trees</li><li>How to care for trees</li><li>Goodness of fuel-saving stoves</li><li>God made us responsible to care</li><li>It is good to promote bee-keeping</li><li>Recommendations are possible to do</li><li>How to care for soil</li><li>Animal care and disease reduction</li></ul>	<ul><li>Build proper housing for goats (7)</li><li>Start a tree nursery (20)</li><li>Do mulching and conservation farming (9)</li><li>Make a fuel-saving stove (9)</li><li>Establish a personal forest</li><li>Establish a community forest</li><li>Make tree guards (12)</li><li>Plant trees either side of the river (5)</li><li>Promote & start bee-keeping (20) – firstly in Kumi Lanjujhi village ("Ten Bees")</li></ul>

CHILEKA ("To leave"): What have you learned/been reminded about? 20 attendees (60% male); 2 funerals clashed on the workshop day;	CHILEKA: What will you do in next 6 months?
• How to care for and protect trees • Spirit of working together • Agroforestry • Trees give us oxygen • How to care for animals • Trees give us food for all • Trees purify air of carbon dioxide • God wants us to care, not destroy creation • Managing trees and animals • Conservation farming • Benefits of fuel-saving stoves • Do not cultivate up to riverbanks	• Continue/expand conservation farming (7) • Plant 1 papaya and 1 mango (15) • Dry and preserve mangoes (6) • Make a fuel-saving stove (10) • Plant 20 trees (10 fruit/10 fodder) • Keep pigs in a proper pen • Share with existing farmer groups

REFERENCES &
FURTHER READING

Ajulu, D. (2001) *Holism in Development: an African perspective on empowering communities.* (World Vision International, 216 pp.).

Batchelor, P.G. and Boer, H.R. (1966) *Theology and Rural Development in Africa.* (Eerdmans, Grand Rapids, USA, 24 pp).

Batchelor, P.G (1969) *Christians & Rural Development.* (Tearfund, UK, 32 pp).

Batchelor, P.G. (1983) *La Terre en Partage - pour un développement à la mesure de l'homme.* (SCAR, Lausanne, 173 pp).

Batchelor, P.G. (1993) *People in Rural Development.* (2nd edn. Paternoster Press, Carlisle, UK, 228 pp).

Boyd, A. (2019) *Neither Bomb Nor Bullet – Benjamin Kwashi: Archbishop on the Front Line - a biography.* (Monarch, Lion-Hudson IP, Oxford, UK, 336 pp.) .

Cassidy, M. (1995) *A Witness for Ever: the dawning of democracy in South Africa.* (Hodder & Stoughton, 236 pp).

Cassidy, M. (2012) *The Church Jesus Prayed For* (Monarch, UK, 415 pp.).

Cassidy, M. (2019) *Footprints in the African Sand: my life & times* (SPCK, London, 471pp.).

Chambers, R. (1983) *Rural Development: putting the last first.* (Longman, London, 246 pp).

Chambers, R. (1997) *Whose Reality Counts?: putting the first last.* (IT Publ, London 318 pp).

Cormack, D. (1987) *Team Spirit: People working with People.* (Marc, Kingsway UK 222 pp).

Evans, D.J., Vos, R.J. & Wright, K.P. - eds. (2003) *Biblical Holism & Agriculture: Cultivating Our Roots.* (William Carey Library, Pasadena CA, USA, 299 pp.).

Gwaivangmin, A.I.T. & Wibberley, E.J. (2003) *Globalisation, Trade and Sustainable Farm Livelihoods. Paper for Micah Network International Consultation,* Querétaro, Mexico, September 2003, 12 pp.+ appendices.

Handy, C.B (1993) *Understanding Organisations.* (Penguin Books, London).

Hirt, H-M & M'Pia, B. (2001) *Natural Medicine in the Tropics* (ANAMED, 158 pp.) .

Jakonda, S.Z.(1998 & 2001, 2nd edn.) *Thy Kingdom Come: a RURCON Manual on Wholistic Development.* (RURCON, Jos, Nigeria, 85 pp).

Joy, D.C. & Wibberley, E.J. (1979) *A Tropical Agriculture Handbook* (Cassell UK, 219 pp).

Kyamuwendo, E. & Wibberley, E.J. (2011) "Farmer Collaboration through FARMS (Farm Asset Resource Management Study) Groups)" pp. 235-244 (Vol.1) In *Thriving in a Global Market: Innovation, Co-operation and Leadership.* International Farm Management Association (IFMA) 18th World Congress, New Zealand (eds. Gardner, J. & Shadbolt, N.). .

Lawrence, J. (2004) *Growing Leaders – reflections on leadership, life and Jesus.* (CPAS/BRF – Bible Reading Fellowship, Oxford, 288 pp.).

Lingenfelter, S.G. & Mayers, M.K. (1986) *Ministering Cross-Culturally* (Baker US 124 pp.).

Maathai, W.M. (2009) *The Challenge for Africa* (paperback edition, Arrow Books, Random House Group, London, 319 pp.).

McCrystal, L. (2005) *The Gift of True Freedom* (ACAT, RSA, 158 pp. https://acatkzn.co.za).

Musa, D. (2009) *Christians in Politics: How can they be Effective?* ACTS (Africa Christian Textbooks) Bukuru, Nigeria, 187 pp.

Oldreive, B. (1993) *Conservation Farming for Communal, Small-scale, Resettlement and Co-operation Farmers of Zimbabwe.* (Rio Tinto Foundation/Organis'n of Collective Co-ops., Zimbabwe, 77 pp.).

Racloz, E. (1977) *Oku Lima: le developpement rural vu à la base.* (Edns. du Soc, Lausanne, Switzerland, 90 pp).

Sanusi, A. (2014) *Gloria! The Archbishop's Wife.* (Release International, 148 pp.).

Schumacher, E.F. (1974) *Small is Beautiful.* (Abacus, London, 255 pp).

Sharland, R. (1992) *The Stewardship of God's World as a Basis for Rural Development Teaching* (OAIC/RDE, Nairobi, Kenya, 28 pp).

Steer, R. (2018 reprint; 1997) *George Müller – Delighted in God* (Christian Focus, 253 pp.).

Stephens, C.O. (1998) *Thinking Communally, Acting Personally* p.61 (ISBN 9 780620 228435).

Struthers, A. (1972) *Instead of the Thorn: story of the Faith & Farm Project.* (SUM, Sidcup, UK, 63 pp.).

Telfer, C. (2006) *Robber of the Cruel Streets [re George Müller]* – book & DVD (CTA, UK).

Venter, A. (2004) *Doing Reconciliation: racism, reconciliation and transformation in the church and world.* (Vineyard International Publishing, Cape Town, South Africa, 407 pp.).

Wibberley, E.J. (1992) "The Farmer-Dominant Study Group: a Practical Paradigm in International Extension Strategy." PhD Thesis, Agricultural Extension and Rural Development Department, University of Reading, 441 pp.

Wibberley, E.J. (2001) "Created Stewards for God's Husbandry: towards a Christian Theology for Agriculture & Rural Development." Master of Theology (MTh) of Brunel University (at London School of Theology) 190 pp.

Wibberley, E.J. (2007) "A Framework for Sustainable Agriculture." pp.125-136 In Berry, R.J.– ed. *When Enough is Enough: A Christian*

Framework for Environmental Sustainability. (Apollos, Nottingham, UK, 213 pp.).

Wibberley, E.J. (2011) *The Case for Creation.* Pamphlet 383, 8 pp. Creation Science Movement, Portsmouth, UK.

Wibberley, E.J. (2014) "Treasuring Trees for Agricultural Management Transformation." *International Journal of Agricultural Management* 3(3) 127-134.

Wibberley, E.J. (2017) "Family Farming Worldwide." pp. 105-120 In *Just Food?* – ed. Barbara Butler (Christians Aware, Leicester, UK, 229 pp.).

Wright, C.J.H.(2010) *The Cape Town Commitment: a confession of faith and a call to action.* Third Lausanne Congress, 80pp. https://lausanne.org and https://dictumpress.com.

Useful websites include:
https://acatkzn.co.za
https://africanenterprise.org
https://anamed.org/en
https://chipspeace.org
https://www.icfem-mission.org
https://www.map.org
https://mcc.org
http://rurcon.org
https://www.tearfund.org
https://www.toughstuffonline.com
https://echonet.org
https://fourthway.co.uk – Regarding fuel-saving stoves - Poster Pack by Bainanga Andrew, Ben Tunstall and Sam Rich (2005). This was co-sponsored in Uganda by a group of NGOs:- ACDI/VOCA, Agromisa, AHI, ASPS, Caritas, Farm Talk, JIDDECO, *Kulika,* EMA, NOGAMU, SACU (Send-A-Cow Uganda), St Jude's, Straight Talk

Foundation. *Kulika* Trust gave it to me and are major users/promoters of this excellent resource.

THE HOOPOE OF HOPE

[Penned at RURCON HQ, Bible Society,
Jos, Nigeria, on 27.11.'04 at 5.30 p.m.]

Searching the ground under fine
Jacaranda – Mango tree backdrop of scene –
Elegant Hoopoe in evening
splendour, no time to perch or to preen.

Sharing the setting, myself, fowl and
dog – Other birds flit through the air –
Distant the rumble of partying
drum-fog; newly, Cassava grows there.

Harvested crop-trash and Zobo stalks
dead, Maize, Sorghum, Okro as well,
These, the surroundings where Bible
is fed - Good news to others to tell.

Thank You, my Father, creation speaks
clear – Ishaku now comes down the road,
Laterite-dusted, a face glowing cheer, with Psalm 91 as his code.

The Hoopoe departed, the Hoopoe of
hope, but left behind hope in the heart;
We don't need in squalor to grovel and
grope with Christ's own assurance as start!

ABOUT THE AUTHOR

Dr John Wibberley is married to Jane and lives in Devon, England. They have two sons and six grandchildren. John committed his life to Christ as a youth. He is an agriculturalist, professor and preacher who has served in integral mission since being mentored by following Peter Batchelor's example from 1966. John and Jane were missionaries with SUM (now *Pioneers*) in Nigeria in the mid-1970s. He served on *Tearfund's* Overseas Development Committee from 1977-1989. In 1989 he stepped down as Head of Agriculture at the Royal Agricultural College, Cirencester to set up REALM (Rural Extension Agriculture Land Management) to enable integral mission work – doing some things for something, some for nothing and some for the normal rate of pay ("tent-making") – thus putting bread on the table. John & Jane testify to over three decades of the Lord's faithfulness to REALM, which included part-time Coordination of the UK Communications Unit of RURCON Africa (http://rurcon.org) from 1996-2013, and working with churches in Christian Stewardship of the Gospel. Assignments have taken John to over 70 countries, especially in Africa, Asia and Latin America, as well as North America, Australia, NZ, Europe and the Middle East. Work has been alongside many integral mission ventures from Africa Co-operative Action Trust (ACAT) Southern Africa, to Inter-Christian Fellowships Evangelical Mission (IcFEM) in Kenya. John has served on a variety of Boards, including *African Enterprise* UK Board since 1995. From 1998-2003, he chaired the UK Farm Crisis Network (FCN) which grew from the Agricultural Christian Fellowship and the National Agricultural Chaplaincy Centre in the UK; he still chairs in Devon the local group in FCN (now Farming Community Network). He is a Trustee of *The Exmoor Society,* having been a Secretary of State appointee to Exmoor National Park in SW England from 2008-2016. He also chairs the Tropical Agriculture Association (https://taa.org.uk) and is a Visiting Professor at the University of Reading and at The Royal Agricultural University, Cirencester, UK. This short handbook is written with eternal gratitude to our Loving and Forgiving God.

ABOUT THE BOOK

Peter Batchelor (1926-2016) took his Christian faith seriously to be applied in practice to every aspect of life, and believed this should be shared accordingly. Thus he was led to spend his life engaged in integral mission, founding *Faith & Farm* in Nigeria in 1958, becoming an early trustee of *Tearfund* UK from 1968, and co-founding RURCON Africa in 1971.

I am really excited about the impact of this book *Approaching Integral Mission*. When the church is committed to *Integral Mission,* it will incarnate the values of the Kingdom of God and witness to God's love and the justice revealed through Jesus Christ. *Integral Mission* enables the church to bring a prophetic word, addressing the whole person, including their physical, social and spiritual needs. By the power of the Holy Spirit, this leads to transformation at all levels - individual, family and community. The task of the local church is to *equip and mobilise men and women for God's mission - integral mission*, not exclusively in the church building, but in ways that will honour the Lordship of Jesus Christ throughout all the diverse fields of human endeavour.

—Andrew Gwaivangmin, Executive Secretary of Nigeria Evangelical Missions Association (NEMA) & former Team Leader/CEO of RURCON Africa.

We celebrate RURCON with you all brothers and sisters, remembering fifty years of reaching and changing the world. We in Africa are grateful for the many activities and shared experiences over the years, and encouragement and prayers. Thanks for the periodicals and Newsletters from RURCON.

> — Bishop Stephen and Rael Kewasis, Kenya – **Bishop Stephen is a past Board Member of RURCON.**

Integral mission is to help people to make their corporate dwelling with Christ for fullness of life now, so that all of it is transformed (farming etc.), so that He will be found and find them again and again.

> — The late Bishop Simon Barrington Ward KCMG speaking in 2008 to RURCON Communications Unit UK Trustees & Advisory Council of which he was Chairman for 30 years from 1980-2010

Integral mission in the footsteps of Jesus Christ inspired the foundation of African Enterprise sixty years ago for evangelisation of the cities of Africa in Word & Deed. The Bible shows that the Gospel addresses whole people, whole relationships through integral mission.

> — Dr Michael Cassidy, Founder of *African Enterprise* & Honorary Co-Chairman of The Lausanne Movement in succession to the late Dr John Stott CBE

My late father, Barnaba Dusu, was motivated to apply the Gospel in every aspect of his Christian life and service, including the co-Founding of RURCON Africa in 1971 to serve the cause of such integral mission across Africa and beyond. He served as RURCON Board Chairman for its first 27 years.

> — Lydia Dusu Trustee of RURCON Communications Unit, UK

Integral mission is central to the approach of the work in which the author and I have served as colleagues and friends during the past three decades. It encapsulates the Biblical foundation of mission in Word & Deed exemplified by the Lord Jesus Christ and that we seek to encourage through the Fellowship of Evangelical Broadcasters.

— Harvey Thomas, CBE, *Fellowship of Evangelical Broadcasters.*

At Inter-Christian Fellowships Evangelical Mission (IcFEM Mission), we strongly and firmly believe and propagate the whole gospel of Jesus Christ in the communities by ensuring that evangelism and social responsibility are the two inseparable sides of the same redemptive power of the Gospel. We believe salvation is for the whole person thus soul, body and spirit and his/her environment. It is the reason as IcFEM we have cherished the mentorship and fellowship in Prof. John Wibberley's great work through RURCON for the last over twenty-five years.

—Solomon Nabie, Mission Director, IcFEM MISSION,
Kimilili, Kenya.

Printed in Great Britain
by Amazon

22594187R00119